# CHOCOLATE DONUT DAYS

## *Life After Breast Cancer*

*Celebrate the*
*Chocolate Donut Days!*
*⌣ Michele*

# Michele Truran Brymesser

Chocolate Donut Days!

# CHOCOLATE DONUT DAYS

## *Life After Breast Cancer*

## Michele Truran Brymesser

*Cover Photo by: Jordan Kelley Brymesser*

# Bras, Boobs, and Biopsies & Feeling Blessed

The moment I found out that my mammogram didn't look good, I began writing. A friend told me writing might help me cope. I kept a journal and shared my writing with others. My stories were very real and full of raw emotion. Any diagnosis no matter the kind, stage, or treatment plan is devastating. Writing helped ease my medical anxiety, and calmed me when I was feeling frustrated with my many emotions as a cancer patient. Cancer rocked my otherwise happy world. At the end of my treatment year, others encouraged me to publish my stories, and *Jelly Donut Days (2016)* was printed. After finishing treatment, I continued to write, finding putting my thoughts onto paper very therapeutic. Even in the sadness that comes with a life touched by cancer, I choose happy. I continue to try to maintain my sense of humor. I hope my stories make you laugh on occasion. I feel so very fortunate to now be cancer-free; and strive to find joy in the simple things, cherish every single moment, and live my life one day at a time. Prayers always appreciated. Let your faith be bigger than your fear.

Warmly, Michele

# Acknowledgements

Sometimes those who help the most do so without even realizing it. They are the people who just know how to "be there." They shuffle about their own lives without ever forgetting to remind you they are there. They find ways both big and small to let you know they care. Their presence helps a family to feel deeply loved. Those people are true friends.

> *They were with me through some of my darkest days, helping me to "keep on keeping on."*
>
> *It is those people to whom I will forever be indebted.*

Also, with my deepest, heartfelt appreciation, I thank each and every one of you who have read my stories, laughed with me, cried with me, and helped to celebrate my happy ending. May God richly bless all of your days, and may your faith always be bigger than your fear. May your lives be filled with the laughter of children, the warmth of family love, the fond memories of the past, and the hope of the future.

# The Wisdom in this Book

*Life is worth celebrating…buy the chocolate donut.*

I dedicate this book to my
husband Mike and our children,
Cody, Morgan, and Jordan.

*You are the sprinkles on all of my donut days.*
*What a joy it is to share life's blessings with you.*

In loving memory of my mom,
who always knew I would
someday write a book.

She would be *really* impressed
to know I've written two.

*Yvonne Eileen Truran*
*February 22, 1935-August 5, 2001*

# *Foreword*
## *from the author's sister*

"Take one day at a time," were the words I said to my sister when I learned that she was battling breast cancer.

I believe everyone has a story and even those with similar stories don't travel down the same path. After facing some life challenges of my own and watching my friends do as well, I hoped that by telling my sister to take one day at a time, it would help her to face what was to come...when it came.

I knew I could be along the side of her path but not on it with her, because this was her story.

In reading this, I hope you remember that everyone has a story. Everyone has gone through something that has changed them.

Remember to always take one day at a time and treasure the moments.

Kelley

*Author's Note: I have the best sister.*

# *Foreword*
## *from the middle child*

As the daughter of the author, I can say that her first book *Jelly Donut Days* is filled with 100% true stories about how cancer affected our family during the year that she was fighting. It was a long, hard year for not only my mom, but for our entire family. I am the middle child, with an older brother and a younger sister. While my mom was as strong and positive as ever, her diagnosis quickly changed our lives. Each of us had specific roles in holding the family together during her illness. I quickly became grocery shopper, cleaning lady, cook, chauffeur, and most importantly a caregiver to the most important woman in my life, my mom.

My mother's diagnosis came at the start of my senior year of high school. I was a busy Varsity Cheerleader, and a newly crowned State Dairy Princess. While my mom was at nearly every single event in which I was involved, it just wasn't quite the same. She didn't want to stop being a mother during her treatments, so she fought to be the best mom possible while she was fighting cancer even harder.

As I reflect on the year I spent by my mom's side, the biggest change I've noticed is how close our family has become. Now we talk more, laugh more, and overall just spend more time together. *Chocolate Donut Days* is the aftermath of the year we spent as caregivers to my mom. It's the truth of what happens after a year of fighting. Hopefully this book brings fewer tears and more smiles and laughs.

Morgan Taylor Brymesser

*Author's Note:*
*To say I'm incredibly proud of this kid would be an understatement!*

# *From the Author*

Someone asked me, "Why another book? What could you possibly write about?" I wasn't sure I had an answer. I suppose it goes a bit like this:

> *I wrote some stories and shared them*
> *during some of my darkest days.*

My friends liked my stories and encouraged me to publish a book that would chronicle my year fighting breast cancer. The internet is a great source of quality self-publishing options that can make ordinary people like me feel like real authors.

> *I published a book. I liked it.*
> *Other people liked it, too.*
> *I kept on writing.*

It was hard for me to understand why those who didn't know us found joy in reading my stories, and I could only assume it was the small tidbit of wisdom at the conclusion of each story.

I told my husband that if only for a moment I wished I could step outside of our lives, pretend I didn't know "us" and decide whether or not *Jelly Donut Days* truly is a good book. Regardless, I feel confident another book is worth publishing.

People who read my stories tell me they feel like they are walking right alongside of us on this path called life.

*Chocolate Donut Days* is a book that celebrates that path. May you strive to find at least one small joy in every single day.

Michele Truran Brymesser

# *After the Beach*

## Monday, August 1

It was on that peaceful day at the beach in late July that I decided I was certain I wanted to publish my book, *Jelly Donut Days: Fighting Breast Cancer, One Day at a Time*. If my story helped even one breast cancer patient and her family feel more *normal* in the midst of their journey it would all be worth my while. It was also the day I concluded writing is very therapeutic for me, and any breast cancer survivor can tell you that we need something therapeutic to help us cope. So, I decided to keep on writing. Chocolate makes everything better, so *Chocolate Donut Days* seemed to be an appropriate title for my second book.

*The wisdom in this story: While I hope to live for many, many more years, if for some reason cancer steals that away, my stories can be passed on for generations.*

# Deadlines and Donuts

**Friday, August 5**

Today I submitted my first book for publication, and I smile to know I am already working on my second book. I was proud to have submitted it on the fifteenth anniversary of my mother's passing. During my cancer year, I lost my stamina for a lot of things. I felt myself muddle through the days, and had an incredible longing to say, *"I'm back."* Just this week, I set an August 5 deadline for myself for publication. I knew it would be a rush, but it felt good to have a deadline and something that required me to be fully focused on something other than *just* cancer.

***The wisdom in this story: "A goal without a plan is just a wish." (Antoine de Saint Exupery)***

# *Senior Discount*

## Saturday, August 6

I went from long hair, to short hair, to shaved hair, to no hair, to stubble, to spiked hair, to short hair, and now — I have *curly* hair. I have never in my life had curly hair, and to be honest, I'm not sure quite what to do with it. I tried parting it on the left — fail. I tried parting it on the right — fail. I finally gave up and brushed it straight back. The curls seemed to fall into place. I asked my youngest daughter how it looked. She is the one who says absolutely what she thinks, *and that's what I love about her.* She laughed out loud and quietly said, "I don't know." Her expression was priceless. Her honesty made me laugh more. I'm about the perfect mix between 1950s greaser look and ninety-year old lady who visits the salon once a week for a set-and-style. I decided my current hair is better than sick and bald, so I embraced my new look. And then it happened…I took my older daughter out to lunch. The twenty-something girl at the register asked me if I qualified for the senior discount. Knowing I am creeping closer to fifty, and never willing to cover the little bit of gray I have earned *(from teenagers, not cancer)*, I smiled and asked, "Oh, what is the age for your senior discount?" *(Knowing some places offer it at 50).* She smiled brightly and said, "Sixty." *Sixty?!?* I said "no thank you," and couldn't help but feel a little insulted. At the age of 48, did I really *look* 60? Some days I *feel* 60, but did I *look* it, too? Then my older daughter, who unlike her younger sister tries to sugar-coat everything, said, "Oh, when I'm at work I offer *everyone* the senior discount!" I answered, "Don't do that anymore!" Exactly one week later, we were shopping and my youngest daughter was contemplating the purchase of one more item. The sixty-something sales lady said, "Well, today's the day to get it — it's senior discount day!" I smiled, tossed the item into the cart, accepted the senior discount and laughed the whole way to the car. My youngest daughter

3

couldn't wait to share the story with the rest of the family and our laughter continued several miles down the road.

*The wisdom in this story: If someone offers you a senior discount — take it! (Even if you're only forty-eight...)*

# *Blooms*

## Monday, August 8

On the day of my last radiation in May, one of the nurses offered to escort me to the car. I know that wheelchair rides out of the hospital are mandatory, so I thought perhaps there was some policy at radiation that helped bring closure to the patient on the last day of treatment. Imagine my surprise when the nurse presented me with a large potted planter. "We don't usually do this," she said. I noticed the tears in her eyes as she said, "you've been so good to us." *(I brought them treats every Thursday – I think they looked forward to Thursdays!)* Good to them...they were good to me! I always say that my health care providers helped give me a whole lot more tomorrows. Anyway, it seems some of the nurses pitched in to buy me this beautiful planter with purple blooms. It was beautiful, *(and sadly I knew I wouldn't be able to keep it beautiful).* My husband and I built a house eight-and-a-half years ago. Every Spring, I buy a large potted planter. I place it between my garage doors, and it's the perfect welcome for those who visit my home. *(For those who read my stories, you may recall there is always dog poop on the front sidewalk).* I dutifully water the planter each May, but by early June it is at the end of the driveway with the trash. I either over-water or under-water, but I can never keep a planter blooming past May. This year my new planter from the nurses was different. May came and went, then June. Every time I returned home, I was greeted by beautiful blooms. July came and brought with it some ninety-degree days — still blooming. It is now August, and my planter is beautiful. I anticipate that the flowers will still look beautiful into Fall. Every now and then, God sends us a reminder of miracles. The simple fact that I kept a planter alive all the way through summer, *for the first time ever* is a miracle.

*The wisdom in this story:*
*"There's a miracle of friendship that dwells within the heart,*
*And you don't know how it happens, or how it gets its start.*
*But the happiness it brings you always gives a special lift,*
*And you realize that friendship is God's most precious gift."*
                                                    *(BJ Morbitzer)*

# *My Mother*

## Wednesday, August 10

There is not a moment that goes by I don't think of my mother, who passed away fifteen years ago. She was a fighter, and memory of her helped me to be strong during my cancer year. While she is never far from my thoughts, she was even closer during my illness. On the quiet days, I thought about her—a lot. I recalled childhood memories I hadn't thought about in years. Words came out of my mouth that sounded like something she might say. The words just poured out onto the pages as I wrote my stories, sometimes with a touch of humor that surely came from her. *She was the best mom.* My daughter leaves for college soon, and I surprised her with one last New York City trip to see *Finding Neverland*. It was our 11th Broadway show, and while I've loved them all, *Finding Neverland* touched me deeply. At the end of the show, Peter was talking to dear Mr. Barrie about his mother. And I quote:

*Peter: It's just; I thought she'd always be here.*

*Mr. Barrie: So did I. But in fact, she is, because she's on every page you write. You'll have her there. Always.*

*Peter: But why did she have to die?*

*Mr. Barrie: I don't know, Peter. When I think of your mother, I will always think of how happy she looked.*

With that, I realized that *my* mother is always with me…on every page I write. I will always question, "but why did she have to die?"

**The wisdom in this story: When I think of my mother, I will always think of how happy she looked.**

# *The Little Boy with Freckles*

**Thursday, August 11**

Often in the summer, teachers get e-mail. Usually they are school district-related, sometimes they are from school supply companies, but very seldom are there personal e-mails during the summer months. Today I received this:

*Dear Mrs. B,*
*Things finally calmed down and I'm able to reach out to you. How is your summer going? It's hard to believe we begin another school year in a few weeks. I'm certainly going to miss you this year. My son has been thriving all summer, being a typical boy and all. So far he has been super blessed with such caring and amazing teachers. Thank you so much for being such a positive influence in his life. He wears his "Tough Kids Wear Pink, I Wear Pink for Mrs. B" shirt and speaks of you still, so I wanted to reach out and let you know we are both thinking about you and hope all is well. He did a "standing ovation" in honor of you at our local breast cancer awareness event this summer. As he stood, I asked him to "sit down, for this is for survivors." He said, "Mom, we have a survivor – Mrs. Brymesser!" Boy did that ever melt my heart. Hugs to you and your family.*

This beautiful note was from the mother of the little boy who stuck his tongue out at the substitute teacher during my absence – the little boy who struggled because his teacher was sick – the little boy who cried when I left and hugged me when I returned – the little boy who melted my heart on the first day of school and whose smile will stay with me all of my days. I was so blessed to be his teacher.

**The wisdom in this story: "So often you find that the students you're trying to inspire are the ones that end up inspiring you." (Sean Junkins)**

# *Tired Old Minivan*

### Friday, August 12

We will soon say farewell to my tired old minivan. My kids were quite small when we bought the van, and it has served us well. People laugh when I say I still love my van. Some rust will prevent it from passing inspection without costly repair, but the motor is still chugging right along. My new car arrives next week, so thankfully I have a few more days to drive my van. Farewell to the broken door, the banged up bumper, and the DVD player we once loved so much. Gone are the days of DVDs and car seats. It's time for back up cameras and navigation. While many people trade vehicles in just a few years or at 100,000 miles, I have owned mine for 13 years and I boast about my 248,000+ miles. Those miles are full of so many years of memories. I think my van's final run will be taking my daughter to college—it seems fitting. While I am sad to see my van go, I am excited about my new vehicle, as it feels like a fresh start. Last year was a challenge in so many ways…a year full of surgeries, chemotherapy, and radiation—a year full of sickness and sadness, with intermittent smiles. This year a new road lies before me. I pray the smiles will be many and the jelly donut days be few. But, no matter what—just like my tired old minivan—I have the strength to keep chugging right along.

*The wisdom in this story: "What lies behind us and what lies before us are tiny matters compared to what lies within us." (Ralph Waldo Emerson)*

# *Band-Aids*

**Thursday, August 18**

When my oldest daughter was a toddler, she stepped on a toy, and got a tiny cut on her foot. She couldn't go to sleep without a band-aid. The band-aid started creeping further up her leg to her knee. Eventually, she found a special spot on her hand that "required" a band-aid. *(There was no boo-boo, but she "needed" that band-aid.)* Band-aids were a comfort to her. She wore one daily through the last day of Kindergarten. The pediatrician told me not to worry — it was better than a dirty old security blanket. I sent her off to college with 100 band-aids. I don't think she is going to need them. She texted last night to say the first day was just great! While it was so very hard to send my daughter to college, she is ready. She stayed close by my side last year during my illness, and now it is her time to shine!

***The wisdom in this story: "Outside of the comfort zone is where magic happens." (unknown)***

# *They Don't Know*

## Wednesday, August 24

It has been said that cancer patients often identify themselves with their greatest pain, because it is also their greatest victory, but I refused to let my cancer identify me. One of the biggest struggles for me last year was becoming known as Mrs. B, first grade teacher — the one with *cancer,* (as opposed to simply Mrs. B, first grade teacher). I am back at school for a new year. Tonight was Open House, a time where parents can visit the classroom with their children to meet the teacher and ease any back-to-school worries. While my short curly hairdo *(that I still don't know quite how to manage)* may make me look like a senior citizen, I no longer really look like a cancer patient. People tell me I look healthy, even vibrant. As each new student entered the classroom this evening, they eyed me with the same curious smiles that new students usually do, but with none of the questioning gazes that I sometimes received from last year's class. The parents looked like any other new-to-first-grade parents, and none looked at me knowingly with what I came to refer to as *sad eyes.* Halfway through the evening, it occurred to me — *they don't know.* These people new to my classroom, some even new to my school, don't know that I have been sick. What a joyful moment, to be Mrs. B, first grade teacher once again. I shook the hands of many, and realized that I need not reach immediately for the hand sanitizer, as my delicate system is no longer immune compromised. I smiled naturally and embraced the thought of these students as *my* new students...not a class I will have to share with substitute teachers. For a brief moment, cancer was not at the forefront of my mind. But, then I saw it, a family lingering by my desk — a student from last year, with his parents — and then another, and another, and another. They had come back to say hello, and with their warm greetings, were reminders of the ways they wrapped me in

11

their love last year and wore pink in my honor. They were reminders of Mrs. B, first grade teacher—the one with cancer. Even so, they brought with them the curious smiles and love only someone who sees you through heartache can offer. While it is nice some people don't know about my illness, I finally accepted that as a cancer survivor, I often identify myself with my greatest pain because it is also my greatest victory. In spite of my best efforts to not allow it, cancer *does* identify me. I can only hope that I am some of the things the parents described me as last night...a fighter, an inspiration, a hero to a child.

*The wisdom in this story: "Your history cannot be erased, but your future has yet to be written." (unknown)*

# *With this Ring*

### Monday, August 29

For as long as I can remember, and until her passing, my mother had a beautiful, filigree and glass top jewelry box that she kept in her top left dresser drawer. I can vividly remember sitting at the edge of her bed, carefully taking out the jewelry box, and playing with her jewelry. Of course, I had mom's permission to do this, as she was the type of mom who believed her things also belonged to her children — nothing was ever too important to not share. There was a wide assortment of jewelry — some vintage clip-on style earrings from the 50s for the lady who never had pierced ears, some long silver chain and charm type jewelry from a home-party company popular in the 70s, and a locket I believe she even had as a child. The item that intrigued me the most though was a beautiful bridal set that included engagement diamond and wedding band. They were white gold, only a little too big for my hands, and incredibly sparkly. I remember touching the *real* diamond and dreaming of someday having one of my own. On a few occasions, I questioned why my mom didn't wear the rings, and her answer was quite simple — they didn't fit. It never occurred to me back then that she could have visited a jeweler to have the rings resized. I think she was too practical to pay for the adjustment, and too optimistic that she would someday lose weight and they would fit again. My mom did lose weight, but by then she was a stage 4 colon cancer patient and confined to a hospital bed. The rings never returned to her finger, and she never asked for them. Shortly after mom's death, and without consideration that he had two daughters, my father sold the rings, *(along with the jewelry box that I so loved)*. My father was financially comfortable, so a quick sale of the rings wasn't really necessary, and his decision will remain something I will never understand…but grief does that to people. It makes you do things you wouldn't normally do, and sometimes it even makes you selfish. Just as I couldn't understand why my father would so quickly get rid of my mother's rings *(and so many other personal belongings)*, he couldn't understand why I felt it was so important to keep these reminders of her. So, it was just yet another time in my adult life my father and I had to agree to disagree. Around that same time, my own beautiful bridal set became too tight. For awhile, I stopped wearing my rings. At first, I was too practical to pay for the adjustment, and too optimistic I would someday lose weight and they would fit again. But then, I decided my rings were too important not to wear. They were a symbol of the commitment to marriage my husband and I share. They were a reflection of years and years of togetherness. I wore these rings on my wedding day as my husband held my hand so delicately. I wore these rings as I proudly cooked dinners in our home as a newlywed. I wore these rings as I rocked our babies to sleep. I wore these rings as I taught our children to sculpt with play-doh. When I did find occasion to remove my rings, my own daughters admired them and played with them as I had once done with my mom's rings. I paid for the adjustment and had my rings resized. I wore them proudly. Then came the cancer. There were lots of hospital visits and the required removal of all jewelry. There was chemo, which seemed to cause every part of my body to swell. My rings no longer fit. I stopped wearing them. I missed them—a lot. Chemo ended, but the swelling did not. Perhaps it was a residual side effect from treatment, perhaps it was the summer heat, perhaps it was my love of the saltshaker—but my hands were swollen. Summer came and went and I missed wearing my rings. As I got dressed for my first day of school, my outfit didn't feel complete without my rings. Push, shove, twist, slide, ugh— my rings remained tight, but I was determined to wear them. I looked at the sparkly diamond and all that it represented. I reflected on the love and care my husband has shown me throughout our marriage, but especially during this cancer year.  We have lived the "for better or worse," and we have lived the "for richer or poorer."  We have lived the "in sickness and in health."  As I thought about our vows, I thought about the last one.  Traditionally, the vow is often written as "'til death do us part," but as a young bride, I hated thinking about dying.  Our final vow, the one my husband and I shared on that day so long ago, was "for as long as we both shall live."

*The wisdom in this story:  I might need to get my ring resized again, because we have a whole lot more living to do.*

# *Still Sore in September*

### Thursday, September 1

One morning in June, I awoke to a very tender breast. My entire breast seemed swollen and sore, especially around the nipple. It reminded me of the exact same feeling I once felt as a nursing mother…when my babies drifted off to sleep and didn't completely empty the breast of milk, engorged. Oh, any mother who has ever nursed a baby knows that feeling. Knowing that feeling came when the milk duct was still full of milk, my mind flashed to where my cancer had started—in the duct. *Please, dear God don't let this be a duct full of cancer that is causing me such pain.* For a brief moment, I didn't know whom to call, as I have so many doctors now—family doctor, breast surgeon, medical oncologist, radiation oncologist, *oh dear*. I decided the breast surgeon would know best, so I called immediately. The sweet nurse in the office told me that it was likely a side effect of radiation, but to be sure the Physician's Assistant would see me. What a shock it was to me that a breast that seemed to have such minimal side effects *during* radiation, was now giving me problems. The Physician's Assistant gave me what I felt was a very thorough breast exam, but even more importantly, treated my worries. She assured me there is never a concern too small, and to *always* call the office if something is bothering me. Once again, I counted my blessings that I have such good medical professionals in my life. A remedy for the pain could be twice a week therapy, a massage to the breast to minimize the fluids around the nipple. At that point, I was feeling "doctored out" and asked if there was any harm in doing nothing. I was told that as long as the discomfort remained minimal, it was fine not to proceed with massage. My husband sweetly offered to take responsibility for the massage duties, which made me laugh. But that's not anything my children (or my readers) care to read about, so we'll just leave it at that. So, it is now

September, and I'm still sore. Not miserable, but it's definitely an uncomfortable feeling that is always with me. I have gotten to the point I don't think about it, but a little fast movement or bend here and there causes me discomfort. I have also noticed I am especially tender at the bra line. I can't even try to figure out the lumps and bumps, because my left breast feels nothing like my "normal" healthy one on the right. So, I will try not to worry, and count the days until my mammogram, when prayerfully a scan will tell me that my discomforts, lumps, and bumps are nothing but simply residual side effects from surgery and treatment.

*The wisdom in this story: One day at a time...*

# *Better Late Than Never*

## Sunday, September 4

In the midst of chemo, I wrote a story called *Pandora (Jelly Donut Days, 2016)*. In that story, I wrote about a special teacher named Mrs. B. She was a middle school English teacher, and taught me much of what I know about being a good writer. I wrote that once my chemo side effects subsided, I wanted to pay her a visit, to offer a long overdue thank you to her. An online search told me that my beloved Mrs. B. was 88 years old, and I had hoped that it wasn't too late for her to enjoy a visit from a former student. She was still living in the same house she had when I was in middle school, which just happened to be in my childhood neighborhood. What a joy it was to drive down the tree-lined streets and reminisce along the way to her house. I called yesterday, inquiring when might be a good time to visit. "Well, when do you want to come?" she asked. I told her that I would be attending early church and could be to her house by around 10AM or 10:30AM. She exclaimed, "Well, that's a little early!" I suggested she tell me the time. She said, "Noon would be swell, we'll have a little bite to eat." I told her not to fuss, and please not to feel she needed to fix lunch. She answered, "Well, we'll see about that." Yes, thirty-five plus years later, I still adore her — my Mrs. B., the teacher who taught me to diagram sentences, but more than anything taught me to believe in myself. In her presence, I didn't feel like the shy, tiny middle school student I really was, but I felt capable of doing anything. I knew she would be proud to know I am now a teacher *(and an author, too!)*. As I pulled into her driveway, she was in the garage, most likely awaiting my arrival. She escorted me into her living room, where a small wooden sign was prominently displayed on a side table. The wording on the sign made me laugh out loud. It said, *"I am silently correcting your grammar."* Yes, this was most definitely my beloved Mrs. B.  When I told her I liked the sign, she disappeared momentarily to retrieve a shirt gifted to her by her granddaughter.  The screen-print was in a kid friendly font and stated:

*Let's eat Grandma.*

*Let's eat, Grandma.*

*COMMAS SAVE LIVES.*

She laughed a hearty laugh and then invited me into the kitchen, where yes — she had prepared lunch.  She had lovingly arranged lunchmeat, cheese, tomatoes, watermelon and deviled eggs on a crystal platter.  The effort she put into lunch made me realize this visit was special to her.  Her daughter and granddaughter joined us at the table, and the conversations flowed freely.  I couldn't help but wonder if she was silently correcting my grammar, but I suppose if she was *(or should that be were?)*, she would be partly to blame for anything I might be lacking.  In the midst of lunch, conversation turned toward my book.  She looked slightly unhappy with me and exclaimed, "Well, I thought I might *get* a copy of your book."  Her smile widened when I told her I brought along a copy, and when I said it was in my purse in the living room, she bounded from her chair before I could even attempt to go get it.  She returned hugging the book tightly to her chest, and said, "I hope you'll autograph it."  I had signed the book before coming, and directed her attention to the story *Pandora* in which she was the feature.  She started to read it, but then asked me to read it aloud.  As I felt my eyes well up with tears, I silently praised God for giving me this moment to let my special teacher know how much I loved her.  Why did it take thirty-five years and cancer diagnosis for me to make this visit happen?  We vowed to stay in touch, and she wrote my name in two places in her address book.  M for Michele, but also T for Truran because, as she stated, *"That's how I'll remember you."*  We talked a long time, and she hugged me tightly when I left. She stood in the driveway waving until my car was out of sight, something my own grandmother used to do. Yes, this was a day the Lord hath made, even if in Mrs. B's world it didn't start until long after 10AM. As I drove around the neighborhood, I continued to reminisce. I saw the childhood homes of my elementary school friends; many whose parents have since moved away or sadly have already passed. I looked at the sidewalks where I used to ride my bike without a care in the world, and longed for just a little bit of the freedom from worry I once felt. If only for the day, I was thankful to once again feel like a middle school student, wrapped in the love of Mrs. B.

*The wisdom in this story: "As long as you're breathing, it's never too late to do some good." (Maya Angelou)*

# *An A+*

## Wednesday, September 7

So she sent a thank you note already…

*Michele,*
*Your visit today was a delight! How can I ever thank you?!? You really made my day--week, month!! I started reading the book this afternoon and you get an A+!! It's very interesting and very well written, (another A+). With your positive attitude I feel sure you will beat your illness and be around for a very long time educating our children and making them happy – as you made me today. We'll be in touch – and again, THANK YOU!!*

*Love, Jackie (Mrs. B.)*

Mrs. B's heartfelt note made *my* day--week, month!! How wonderful to have the privilege of reconnecting with someone after so many years. I will make every good effort to stay in touch with this sweet lady in the years to come.

**The wisdom in this story: "No distance of place or lapse of time can lessen the friendship of those who are thoroughly persuaded of each other's worth." (Robert Southey)**

# *The Elephant in the Room*

### Thursday, September 8

Tonight was Back to School Night at my school, a night where teachers present curriculum and classroom policies to the new parents and former parents stop in to say hello. This year, I felt it necessary to add a few slides to my usual slide show presentation. Immediately following a beautiful picture of my family is a clip art of a big cartoon elephant. The slide reads:

*The Big Elephant in the Room*
Everyone sees it.
Everyone wonders about it.
People whisper about it.
No one wants to ask about it.
But, it's okay to talk about it.

The next slide reads:

*Yes, I am the teacher who had breast cancer last year.*
I was diagnosed with breast cancer on October 6.
I had surgeries, chemotherapy, and radiation.
I completed my treatments on May 2.
My first scan will be at the end of September.

And the next:

*The love and support I received from my
school family will never be forgotten.*

Finally,

*But that was last year.*
My doctors call me a survivor. My energy levels
have returned, and it is good to be back. Our school
is a great place to be and I'm ready for a new year.

I saw a few tears in the room, some warm smiles, and a few parents who were awkwardly uncomfortable and chose to look away. Once again, I see what cancer can do to people. Simply hearing the word can be hard. While I felt good that there was no longer a big elephant in the room, I wondered if I had done the right thing by sharing. Moments after the parents left for the evening, I sat down to catch up on a few e-mails. It was then that I realized I had done the right thing by sharing my story. An e-mail from a mother follows:

From:           *A First Grade Parent*
To:             *Mrs. Brymesser*
Subject:        *Tonight*

*I just wanted to thank you for your time tonight to explain the first grade curriculum. On a personal note, I want to congratulate you on being a breast cancer survivor. I was very touched to see that you were diagnosed on October 6. My mom passed away from breast cancer on October 6, 1991 when I was a freshman in high school. It was a very sentimental moment for me tonight but thank you for being a fighter and sharing your story.*

Cancer affects so many people in so many ways. I am thankful this mom reached out to me with her personal story. I am thankful medical advances since 1991 have improved, so my daughter didn't have to deal with such a loss during her freshman year of high school. I am thankful while I am once again simply Mrs. Brymesser, first grade teacher, my story will remind others of the importance of breast cancer research.

**The wisdom in this story: I will never, ever stop praying for a cure.**

# *Spa Day*

## Sunday, September 11

My daughter turned eighteen last week, and I wanted to celebrate in a special way. We spent the day at the spa, treating ourselves to chocolate manicures. While the manicure was nice, the best part of the experience was that we got to spend the whole day in fluffy bathrobes lounging in the quiet room, the whisper room, the aromatherapy room, and the outdoor gardens. We even ate lunch at an exquisite buffet…in our bathrobes. I didn't want the day to end. I spent some time reading *Jelly Donut Days* (I am my own worst critic!), while my daughter spent some time reading a novel for her college literature class. My five senses never felt more alive as I looked at all of the beauty around me, savored the quiet, smelled and tasted the chocolate, and felt the warm touch of my manicurist as she gently took my worn hands in hers and slathered them with sweet scents. Aside from reading my book, I didn't really think about cancer, but instead felt so blessed to be alive and enjoying such a wonderful day with my daughter. It was only when we finally retreated to the locker room at the end of the day I was reminded of my illness. As we carefully opened our combination lockers, I looked at my daughter's clothing, neatly folded in her locker. Earlier that morning, I had tossed mine right inside, much like I did for my medical procedures and 34 radiation treatments—tossed in the locker, slightly rebellious, refusing to use the hanger and embracing my get-me-in, get-me-out attitude. It was only then in this place of solitude and comfort I realized my life is still stress-filled. My treatment days are over, and it's time to relax.

***The wisdom in this story: I need another spa day.***

# *Just Because I Can*

**Thursday, September 15**

One of the worst things about being a cancer patient was not being able to do everything I wanted to do for and with my children. More than anything, I wanted to just be "mom." In spite of my illness, I was quite proud to be able to make it to most of their events; perhaps the most challenging being a Florida trip in the midst of chemotherapy, and a New York City trip during radiation. It was on those trips, that I experienced the true compassion of others.

On the Florida trip, I felt an immediate camaraderie with another mom whose health issues also required her to use a motorized wheelchair, which I preferred to call a "wheelie car." We had a wheelie car race in the park with the girls cheering us on, and I laughed until I cried. She bought me a bottle of water, which quenched my thirst, and warmed my heart. I will always have a special spot in my heart for her.

On the New York City trip, another mom and I crossed paths at our favorite macaron store — we were too early, the macarons were not ready yet — come back later. I knew that the rest of my travels with my girls did not include a return trip to the store, as we had a lot of ground to cover, and my energy levels were low. After a busy afternoon, we rejoined the school group for dinner. There on the table, my macaron friend had placed the most perfect box of freshly made macarons…"for you", she said as she smiled brightly.

Tonight was Back-to-School Night for my youngest daughter. She is a sophomore in high school, and suffice it to say that because of her older siblings, this would be my seventh high school Back-to-School Night. It's a fast paced event, and even the healthiest parents find the night literally exhausting.

We are allotted just a few minutes between classes and follow our child's rigorous schedule for shortened periods throughout the evening. I really didn't want to go. My husband offered to go, and I contemplated *(only briefly)* staying home. No, this was a two-parent event. It was something my husband and I had done, without fail, since Kindergarten for each and every one of our children. It didn't matter that it was our seventh high school Back-to-School Night. It didn't matter that it was a fast paced event and I was exhausted before it even started. It didn't matter that I really didn't want to go. What mattered was that just one short year ago I was on the couch, wishing I could go and do all of these things—every single thing. So, off we went. At times, my body ached and I questioned myself, *"Why did I even come?"* and without even a second thought, I answered, *"Just because I can."* I arrived home to a surprise on my front porch—a beautiful note from my NYC friend, and the most perfect box of freshly made macarons.

**The wisdom in this story: On the hardest of days, the kindness of others is inspiring, and gives me strength to do everything I want to do—just because I can...**

# *Sleepless Nights*

## Friday, September 23

I am struggling. My joint pain is greater than I wish to acknowledge during the day. At night, I become restless, and my sleep is interrupted. I am still lumpy, bumpy, and sore. I am frustrated, and I am tired. *I am so very tired.* Sometimes I think that no amount of sleep could cure the tiredness I feel. I want so very much to sleep, but as always, it's in the quiet of the night that my fears surface. I'm just a few days away from going for my first post-treatment mammogram, and I am hopeful after that I will calm down a bit. I can handle the joint pain during the day; I can handle the restless nights; I am even learning to tolerate the lumpy, bumpy, and sore. I just want to hear someone say everything looks good.

*The wisdom in this story: I just want to hear the words cancer-free. Only then, will my mind truly be able to rest.*

# *A Lesson in Patience*

**Tuesday, September 27**

Mammogram Day!  The day for which I had anxiously awaited finally arrived.  I arrived at the imaging center; feeling comfort in knowing a friend would be performing my mammogram.  Her first question for me was, "Where are your previous scans?"  Uh-oh.  It seemed that I was supposed to bring them.  No one told me.  Or had they?  Perhaps, like everything else these days, I had forgotten.  A quick text to my friend who worked at the other imaging center *(gosh, I have a lot of friends in the mammo business!)* and my husband was sent en route to retrieve CDs of my previous images.  He dutifully returned quickly, and passed off the disks, only to be told there was nothing on them.  More texting to my friend — yes, she was certain the images were on the disk.  No explanation, but happy to provide a second copy.  Back to the imaging center he went again, more waiting.  Other patients came and went, all with positive mammogram results whispered quietly in the waiting room, which made me happy.  I know healthcare workers must whisper to respect patient privacy, but I think a good result should be shouted enthusiastically.  Finally, I was alone in the waiting room, my eyes scanning the less than perfect décor — pretty enough, but could be better.  Someone needed to dust the artificial flower arrangement.  The reading material was outdated, with the exception of my own *Jelly Donut Days* book displayed prominently on the table with "waiting room copy" written across the front.  Once again, I was reminded of how much I despise wearing a hospital gown and being in a medical facility.  Yes, I was grumpy at best, but managed to smile at everyone who was trying to work on my behalf to find the prior scans.  Eventually, the second imaging center found a way to upload disks to their system and then transfer images to the appropriate software, certainly too technical for me.  My 3D

Diagnostic Mammogram was done efficiently, and with great care.  My friend and I both had tears in our eyes.  This is hard. I hugged the doctor when he shared my good clean result. My 4-hour visit to the imaging center was over.

*The wisdom in this story:  My husband is an excellent courier.*

# *Rose-Colored Glasses*

**Friday, October 7**

Yesterday was a hard day.  It was exactly a year ago yesterday I heard the words "there are some cancer cells," and later more clearly "you have cancer." *Oh, how those words can change a life.* I remember a friend telling me shortly after diagnosis that I picked a hell of a month to get sick---there is pink everywhere. *I hated the pink.* I have been struggling this week, sometimes frustrated with people, and most definitely trying not to fall into a puddle of tears as I reflect back on my year.  I think I still see the world through rose-colored glasses, which I suppose is a blessing. I really wish others could do the same.  It's hard to let the little things bother me, and I become easily annoyed when I hear others complaining about the small stuff; my picture is bigger.  My picture is about simply being happy to feel healthy, being able to function beyond my cancer rotation of chair, couch, and bed. I seem to have an incredible amount of compassion, also a blessing.  I have a friend whose loved one was recently diagnosed with cancer.  Just yesterday, as I was remembering my diagnosis, my heart was aching for her.  I asked how her loved one was doing.  "Tired."  My friend didn't seem very compassionate and went on to say (about her loved one) "She's just tired every day.  They went for a car ride, and she came home tired.  She is just always tired."  I smiled empathetically, but I wanted to say, "been there, done that."  I wanted to say; "Surgery made me tired, pain pills made me tired, and even a car ride made me tired. As much as I never wanted to admit it, I was a little depressed about my situation and sleeping was the only time cancer wasn't the only thing on my mind--until it started coming to me in the form of nightmares."  I wanted to say, "love her, embrace her, just be there in ways your loved one doesn't even know she needs you."  As a cancer patient, it's perfectly fine to say that you are *tired.*  On a happier note, my scans last week looked good and I don't need to go back until April. I'm counting my blessings...every single day.

*The wisdom in this story: If you are not a cancer patient, please know that offering support goes well beyond wearing a cute pink sweatshirt. Sometimes you have to put on the rose colored glasses, too and view life a little differently.*

# *Pain in the Port*

**Sunday, October 9**

I think I love to complain. I was offended when someone called it "dwelling on my cancer," so I won't say I dwell, but I will say I love to complain. There is so much about this past year that makes me angry. There is so much about how I feel right this very moment that still isn't my *normal*. I'm not happy about it, and sometimes I want to speak it loudly. To dwell, would be to talk non-stop about it, which I don't do. However, what I do is briefly mutter the ugly words, add the voice of self-sorrow, and then move on. *"I hate this port,"* or *"I hate this <u>damn</u> port,"* is something my husband has surely grown tired of hearing. I hated the news that I needed a port. I hated getting the port. I hated having the port. I hated getting the port removed, and now—I hate the scar that remains. With the surgery to implant the port, my stitches didn't dissolve completely and the incision never healed correctly. When they removed the port, a small stitch protruded from the incision, and again it didn't appear to heal correctly—and it bothers me. At first, I truly thought it was all in my mind, the pain I felt after the port was removed. My port removal was five months ago. It's hard to describe the sensation I feel in the area of the incision. At times, it's like a prickling, almost as if someone is poking me with a pin. At other times, it's a sharp twinge that even hurts, but only for a moment. Sometimes, it's just the dullest of aches. It's not something I've mentioned to my doctor, because to be honest, I'm simply done with procedures. To mention it might make someone think it would be wise to cut it open again and, well—let's just say that's far from anything that interests me. So, when I couldn't sleep, I did a quick online search. I discovered many share my discomfort. There are no answers.

**The wisdom in this story: This is my new normal.**

# *Pink Tears*

## Monday, October 10

Weeks ago, I was invited by my oncology office to be their guest at a breast cancer conference. It was a hard decision for me to accept the invitation, as it required me to take a personal day from school on a previously scheduled staff in-service day. However, one session topic interested me greatly: *Living with the Fear of Recurrence.* Fear, as defined in the dictionary is "a distressing emotion aroused by impending danger, evil, pain, etc., whether the threat is real or imagined; the feeling or condition of being afraid." I pondered this description at great length, especially the part *"whether the threat is real or imagined."* Is the threat of cancer recurring for me real or imagined? My surgeon, oncologist, and radiation doctor all tell me there is only a small chance of recurrence following treatments I received. Oh, how I pray they are right. With every clean scan I know my confidence will grow. However in the meantime, I hoped attending the conference and educating myself about breast cancer would be beneficial. The event venue was a beautiful hotel not far from my home. I arrived early, and parked in the parking garage. Moments later, I found myself on an elevator surrounded by ladies wearing various shades of pink. *I hate pink, but I was wearing pink, too.* They were smiling and appeared happy and healthy. I still looked like a sick person trying to recover. As we stepped off the elevator, I felt alone and frightened. Fear, whether real or imagined, was filling me as I felt my heart beat faster. I wanted to get right back on the elevator and go home, but I knew I needed support. I wasn't prepared for the hallway of vendors and sea of pink that followed. As I walked through the crowded corridor, my eyes filled with tears. When I finally reached the hotel lobby, I couldn't stop crying. I found a comfortable velvet chair and rested in quiet contemplation. This was going to be a hard day. I went into the opening session and found a seat a few rows from the front. I sat down beside an enthusiastic lady who seemed to want to talk. Under normal circumstances, I'm always comfortable talking to a stranger, but here I felt more vulnerable. I wanted my privacy. I wanted to just sit and listen. My bag held several copies of my *Jelly Donut Days* book. I brought them along to give to presenters and other patients I may meet throughout the day. One book was atop the pile, title visible. The lady beside me exclaimed, "Oh—you have *that* book!" I wanted to ask her if she had heard of it, but at that exact moment I liked being anonymous. I quietly answered, "Yes" and secretly hoped she wouldn't ask if it was a good book. To be honest, I'm not sure if it is—but that's another story for another day. The session was informative and overwhelming at the same time. I took copious notes and I think the enthusiastic lady beside me realized I wasn't too into talking. The research regarding 3D mammogram technology was encouraging—early detection leading us one step closer to a cure. I felt quite pleased to know I had chosen the 3D mammogram when it was offered to me, as that is entirely how my cancer was detected. After the opening session, I attended a session whose presenter* wore a pink business suit, a pink feather boa, and a red clown nose. She was a cancer survivor and reminded us it is our responsibility to take control of our recovery path. She told us where we were a year ago is different—it's a process—we have choices. She reminded us to find a bit of laughter in every day. As she finished her presentation, she gave each of us a red clown nose and encouraged us to laugh out loud. We moved on to a pink ribbon luncheon, where my eyes were immediately drawn to the bright smiles of three ladies who looked quite healthy. I later learned two were cancer patients just starting treatment and one was a caregiver. As I watched them enjoy their lunches, I picked at the food in front of me and realized that even after all of these months post-treatment foods don't taste quite right to me. We exchanged the usual pleasantries and as expected, the conversation turned to cancer. I shared as much as I could without frightening them, but remembered to "keep it real" so I didn't mislead them into believing it was going to be easy. When I presented each with one of my books, they were incredibly grateful and told me I was an inspiration. They asked if I would personalize and autograph the books, and when I pulled out my pink and green pens I decided maybe I did like pink—*but only a little.* I left lunch with a lighter heart and a smile on my face, but all of that joy came crashing down when I entered the next session. It was the session I had most looked forward to attending, *Living with Fear of Recurrence.* I arrived just as the presenter was getting started, and the only available seat was in the front row, directly in front of the podium. The presenter** was a doctoral candidate, researcher, and most importantly a cancer survivor. During most of the session, I felt as if she was speaking directly to me. As tears fell from my eyes, I was slightly embarrassed by my behavior. I couldn't see those seated behind me, but suspected I might be the only one in the room who had used the very last tissue in my pocket-sized tissue pack. The session was incredibly informative and thought provoking. I learned FCR (Fear of Cancer Recurrence) is defined as, "fear, worry, or concern relating to the possibility the cancer may come back." The level of fear falls along a spectrum. Some people have natural, healthy concerns about cancer recurrence, and yet for others it disrupts their daily activities and becomes chronically disabling to the point they have a hard time living their lives. I'm pretty certain I fall somewhere in the middle. Cancer is a life changing experience, and for those who haven't had cancer, it's hard to understand all of the different ways survivors worry about cancer coming back and affecting us again. As women, we have many roles and strive to do them all the best we can. Suddenly we feel like we can't. That's very challenging. I learned that we often feel like we're letting someone down, when in reality, it's ourselves we're letting down. Others don't realize how much fear of recurrence and simply reflecting on how cancer has touched our lives affects us. They seem to think we are fine now that treatment has ended. In reality, we are not *fine*. While we celebrate being survivors, we will have some degree of worry about cancer for the rest of our lives. Some people even feel that if they worry, they will be prepared if the cancer does return. The presenter stressed that we need to build trust and rapport with someone with whom we can talk to when we are feeling overwhelmed. Just as I was beginning to feel anxious, the session ended and I thanked the lady in pink shoes for reaffirming that all of my feelings were perfectly normal. The day ended with a closing survivor reception, both heartwarming and encouraging. As each survivor stood to be recognized, I realized I find comfort in knowing there are so many who have been able to put their worst awful behind them. My heart aches for those still fighting. Most ladies departed from the hotel in groups, but I had pretty much stayed solo throughout the day. As I walked to the parking garage, I felt alone again. However, I won't be alone next year. The sweet ladies at lunch suggested we exchange contact information and one already sent me a message. She called me her Pinky Sister, a term I had never heard before today. I wonder if I told her how much I dislike pink? As I traveled home, I replayed bits of the presentations over and over again in my mind. The presenters had most definitely made a huge impact on my life. I was reminded of a special poem shared. I'll leave it here as my wisdom.

**The wisdom in this story:**
> **"She stood in the storm and**
> **when the wind did not blow**
> **she adjusted her sail."**
> **(unknown)**

\* *Tammy Miller, Tammy Speaks, LLC*
\*\**Laura Samuelsson, MS, Doctoral Candidate, UPMC*

# *The Box*

## Thursday, October 27

Being busy is so good for me.  When I am busy, I don't "think."  When I do "think," I think about cancer.  It is still so very hard not to think about the past and feel a little afraid of the future.  When I remind myself, I am able to live in the moment, and that's when I do best.  The Health and Wellness Committee at my church *(in response to five church members being diagnosed with breast cancer in the past year)* consulted with me about ideas for a comfort basket to be given to newly diagnosed patients.  Would I like to help?  *Of course I would like to help!* I met with the coordinator, and she already had some lovely ideas of her own.  Together, we came up with a list of items to include, and I told her I would be happy to assemble a sample basket to display at our upcoming Missions and Ministry fair.  As I meticulously used the label maker to create dividers for a (pink) health notebook, I laughed a little to think of my own disarray of health related paperwork that I have no desire to organize.  As I carefully tied a pink ribbon onto a package of truffles, I smiled to remember how I never lost my taste for sweets during chemo.  As I slipped a copy of my book and a donut shop gift card into a cellophane bag, I wondered how I ever got through my ordeal without more "jelly donut days."  As I added a prayer shawl to the basket, I was reminded of how I got through my ordeal without more "jelly donut days" — it was because I was wrapped in the prayers of so many.  Then it came time to add the final piece to the sample basket…a head covering.  The coordinator of the gift baskets plans to order a bandeau for each basket, and I told her I could provide one for the sample basket.  I procrastinated until late in the evening when I finally asked my husband to reach the box of hats and head-coverings from my closet shelf.  It had not been touched since my daughter placed it there for me last April.  When we put the box on the shelf in April, I said a silent prayer *(okay, a very loud prayer)*, that I would never need to open it again. Yet, this wasn't really going to be a big deal. I wasn't opening the box because I *needed* a hat; I was opening the box as part of a project I was working on for church. I wasn't prepared for the flood of emotions as I lifted the lid off the box. Once again, I sat on my vanity stool in the bathroom, gasping for breath as sobs emerged from deep inside me. My dear husband once again looked bewildered and had no way to "fix things." I looked at the loosely knit department store hats that I had purchased in every available color…the ones that covered my head without making me too warm. I looked at the bandeaus I loved to hate…I loved the versatility and the colors, but hated how they always felt like they were falling off my head. I looked at the pastel pink hat so very carefully knit by a co-worker's mother…the one forever imprinted on my Drivers' License photograph…again, damn you licensing center for not allowing chemo patients to use an old photograph. *Okay, so maybe it isn't forever imprinted, but it will be on the license I carry until February 2020.* Finally, I looked at the bandeau my daughter purchased for me on her trip abroad while I was sick. Of all of the souvenirs she could have brought home, she thoughtfully and selflessly selected something so very personal just for me. Finally, in search of something add to the church basket, I pulled a pink bandeau that I had never worn from the box. *I had such trouble then embracing the color pink – and I still do!* Just as quickly as I pulled it out, I put it back inside and mumbled, "the sample basket doesn't have to include a hat." I continued to cry, and put the lid back on the box. My husband took it from my grasp just as one big teardrop fell on the lid. I thought I was okay. I thought this was all over, but somehow I am still very fragile. The most subtle of reminders sneak in and I am right back in a place that was once my worst awful. It was only then I realized today's date. My first surgery was exactly one year ago today.

*The wisdom in this story: Time will heal all wounds, even the emotional scars that live on in cancer patients.*

# *All that Glitters*

## Saturday, October 29

Today was my youngest daughter's sophomore Homecoming Dance. My baby...the little girl who sucked her thumb for forever; the little girl who crawled in my bed each morning to watch Curious George long after most of her friends stopped watching local public television; the little girl who said nary a word to others, but was loud and free-spirited at home. Yes, she will always be my baby, but I realized tonight just how much my daughter has grown up in the past year. She is tall and tiny, and ordered a gold sequin dress online. Her sister took her shopping for shoes, because as you may recall, I hate the mall. She tried the dress and shoes on at home, and looked quite nice. She looked like my little tomboy girl in a pretty dress. I took her to get a manicure and pedicure, something she has always enjoyed, and then dropped her off at a friend's house to "get ready." Getting ready for Homecoming is quite a lengthy process. I think much of the day involves talking, giggling, and just being teenage girls; but it also involves hair straightening and makeup, something my daughter doesn't usually spend time doing. When her father, sister and I arrived later to take photographs, I was not prepared for what I saw. My daughter looked absolutely stunning. Her golden locks were straight and silky, her eye makeup done to perfection, and she wore the prettiest shade of lipstick—dark pink but not quite red. The thing I liked best was her confidence, and she wore it well. My daughter, who once disliked being the center of attention, smiled broadly for the cameras. She and her two friends (also quite stunning) looked like supermodels. The parents tossed compliments about freely, and the girls smiled even more brightly. I will always hate cancer for stealing away the past year, but as my oncologist told me, "look how many years you gained." Yes, I am here to see this—my daughter, growing from a young girl into a young lady — a transformation that is happening right before my eyes.  I am so very blessed.

*The wisdom in this story:  All that glitters really is gold.*

# *Pennies in the Fountain*

## Sunday, October 30

One of my best memories of time spent with my mother was throwing pennies into fountains.  When I was young, there was a two-story mall we frequented; it had a tall indoor fountain that reached the second story.  There just happened to be an ice cream store across from the fountain, and every trip to the mall included an ice cream cone on the bench, *(mint chocolate chip with chocolate sprinkles)*, followed by throwing pennies into the farthest depths of the fountain from high above.  My mother was a dreamer, and as the pennies flew from my hands she always reminded me to make a wish.  When my son was quite small, and shortly after my mother's first surgery for Stage 4 colon cancer, we shopped at a large establishment that had rainforest-like décor.  They served ice cream and had a bench near the fountain, so of course it became a favorite place.  As my son's chubby hands grabbed penny after penny from my mother's outstretched hand, I smiled to know that fountains would also be a memory for him.  My middle daughter giggled from her stroller as she watched it all, and my youngest was still just one of my many wishes and dreams.  Sadly, she wasn't born in time to experience fountains with my mom.  At some point in my life I stopped wishing on birthday candles, and the same became true for pennies in fountains.  I still always stop and throw pennies, but seldom if ever do I make a wish.  During the month of October, the PA Breast Cancer Coalition dyes the fountain at the Pennsylvania State Capitol pink in honor of breast cancer awareness.  I wanted more than anything to throw pennies in that pink fountain.  A late Sunday morning after church seemed like the perfect time to visit, without the crowds and traffic commonplace in the city on a weekday.  So, today, I stood with my oldest daughter, admiring the beauty of the fountain.  The pink was just perfect in color, dark at the base of the fountain and somewhat cotton candy colored as it rose high into the air. The city was quiet, and as the fountain trickled down, some tears trickled down my cheeks. Life is so very precious. So often in the hustle and bustle of every day life, we forget to stop to appreciate the blessings around us. My very talkative daughter became speechless as we both stared at the beauty of the fountain and enjoyed listening to the trickling of water. After a long stretch of silence, I realized that I had no coins in my wallet. I sent my daughter to the car, where she retrieved three shiny pennies for the fountain. I spent a long time looking at the dates on the pennies, and when she asked me what I was doing, I realized that was a penny ritual I had done for as long as I could remember. 1978, 1984, and 2013—I stopped to reflect briefly on what I was doing during those years. In 1978, I was ten years old…my favorite age. *I cried the night before my 11th birthday when my mother told me I would never be ten again!* In 1984, my uncle (*my mother's brother*) passed away, and it was my first experience with losing a loved one. And 2013…that year stumped me. What was I doing in 2013? Oh, yes, I was feeding the football team. It was one of my best mom-moments, my son's senior year of high school. For some reason, when it was time to throw the pennies into the fountain, I felt hesitant. I told my daughter to throw them. I told her she had better aim than me. She aimed for the top. I chuckled a little, because I always aimed for the bottom. She fell just short of the top. She aimed again and fell short. Finally, she said that she wanted to throw the penny right into the waterfall around the base…she wanted to see it fall. As we walked away, I realized I didn't throw any pennies, but that's okay, my wishes and dreams for the moment have all come true; I am cancer-free and able do most of the things I couldn't do during cancer treatment.

**The wisdom in this story: I wonder if a breast cancer cure is too big of a wish for pennies in the fountain.**

# *Three Rakes and a Broom*

## Sunday, November 13

I grew up in a beautiful neighborhood with sidewalks and tree-lined streets. One of my best memories of childhood was making piles of leaves and jumping in them. The crunch of leaves beneath my boots on a chilly fall morning still brings a smile to my face. My father, who was quite meticulous about his yard, raked those leaves endlessly. Our yard was free of every single leaf, and he fretted over the occasional one that would blow into our yard from a neighbor's property less tidy than ours. My father took great pride in gathering the leaves and securing them snugly in big black garbage bags. Years later, our neighborhood made an effort to be more environmentally responsible, and my father took that same pride in sweeping the leaves to the curb for street collection. He wanted them gone—every single leaf. When I got married, my first home was surrounded by beautiful trees, which meant leaf piles in the fall. My husband tried to rake them *(a job I despise),* but in the countryside we didn't have neighbors to worry about, so our efforts were sometimes minimal. Our kids made piles and jumped in the leaves, and the base of our swing set sliding board became a favorite place to allow the leaves to accumulate. When we built our new home, my husband, who had by then grown tired of mowing around the trees and raking each fall, politely requested that we not plant a lot of trees. We agreed on a flowering cherry, a dogwood, and a flowering pear tree. Nothing more. We told our landscaper we wanted low maintenance. Our children were growing older and didn't really seem to miss jumping in the leaves, and my husband certainly didn't miss raking them. We have lived here almost nine years, and while I enjoy seeing the trees in the mountain behind my home change colors each fall, I haven't really thought much about the leaves, *or lack of,* in my own yard. I don't even think we own a rake.  This morning I left home early enough to be on time for church, and for those who read my stories, you know that on time for church doesn't happen often; I was quite proud of myself.  At an intersection near my home, a big dump truck pulled into my path.  I wasn't happy, because I was certain I had been at the stop sign first, and I *really* wasn't happy because now it was likely that I'd be late for church, *as usual.* Just as I fretted over the truck in the same way that my father used to fret over a stray leaf in the yard, I remembered a time last year when I heard others complain about traffic.  I remembered being envious, because waiting in traffic meant that one was actually well enough to leave the house, something I longed for daily during chemo.  I remember taking a silent vow that I would never again complain about traffic.  So, today instead of cursing this slight delay to my schedule, I smiled and followed the dump truck.  The dump truck had a storage type rack which held three rakes, a broom, a large container of what appeared to be weed killer, and a lawn spreader one might use in the spring.  Such an interesting combination — things for both fall and spring.  I wondered if perhaps this dump truck driver lacked a storage facility or if he simply liked being prepared for all seasons.  As I followed the truck, a single yellow leaf, one that appeared to be dancing in the wind, momentarily distracted my eyes. More leaves followed, almost as if they were tantalizing the driver of the dump truck.  I thought about all of those leaves that are somewhat elusive — the ones that no one can ever seem to capture.  What happens to those leaves?  Well, I'm no environmentalist but I have learned enough to know that they eventually disintegrate.  As I continued to follow the *very slowly moving* dump truck, my mind turned to cancer, and I longed for the day when cancer isn't still at the forefront of my mind.  Cancer cells, like those fall leaves, can quickly multiply and sometimes seem elusive.  My cancer cells were removed by my very own three rakes (surgery, chemotherapy, and radiation), those rakes guided by the most skillful of doctors.

But as everyone knows — even the most careful cleanup with a rake requires the finishing touches of a broom — and I suppose that's just where I am at this moment. I am pushing the broom. I will take a daily medication for five years, a weed killer of sorts, to prevent any residual cancer cells from growing. Without the estrogen they need, the cancer cells *(like the leaves)* will disintegrate. For now, the joint pain and sleepless nights are simply part of the process. In the meantime, I'll do all that I can to spread joy in the lives of others, and continue to pray for a cure for all cancers. I will show kindness toward others, even the dump truck driver who thought he was first. It is easy to forgive him though, as somehow I arrived three minutes early for church.

*The wisdom in this story: I am prepared for all seasons.*

# *The Donut Tree*

### Sunday, November 20

It is our family tradition to get a Christmas tree on the weekend following Thanksgiving. I always love watching my husband carefully string the lights and weave a thin silky red ribbon decoratively through the branches. We have used the same red ribbon on every Christmas tree since we were married. This is our 23rd married Christmas together. Years ago, I chose red and silver glass balls to adorn the tree. As they became broken through the years, I replaced them with durable, yet pretty acrylic ones. My children each have their own box of "special" ornaments that they place on the tree. Although I have friends who display multiple trees in their homes (some have one in almost every room), we have always been a one-tree household. However, today on a stroll through a favorite store, my youngest daughter and I discovered donut ornaments — pink *and* chocolate frosted. These were too perfect to pass up, yet would seem misplaced on our tree with predominantly red and silver décor. We thought perhaps an ornament stand would be appropriate, selected one, and left the store quite proud of our purchases. The donut tree is now displayed on the bar counter in my kitchen. It can be seen from most every angle of the downstairs entertaining area. To infrequent guests, the donut tree may seem distasteful, but friends and loved ones know there is a much deeper meaning. Pink is a color that represents breast cancer awareness for everyone. For me, the pink donut represents my cancer year. It is accompanied by a chocolate frosted donut to balance things out.

*The wisdom in this story: Gosh, I love donuts!*

# *Dear Every Cancer Patient*

**Monday, November 21**

I have a dear friend who is a nurse. For a time, she worked for a local hospice, and I always thought about what an incredible blessing she must have been to the families she served. She has certainly been a blessing to me. She is the friend who consistently says the right thing, does the right thing, and even when she is without words her eyes glisten with compassion. So, imagine my surprise when my friend sent me a blog entry that has been circulating on social media. The blog entry was written by a nurse, and the title is *Dear every cancer patient I ever took care of, I'm sorry. I didn't get it.* The author wrote that after a lengthy career in oncology, she thought she "got-it." She thought she really knew what it felt like to go through a cancer journey — until her own diagnosis. It was an incredibly powerful read. The author so very eloquently put into words all I have been feeling this last year. My friend who sent it — she is one of my friends who truly does "get it." She was a blessing to me on some of my hardest days. I think I might need to remind her.

*The wisdom in this story: How blessed we are to have special people in our lives who never stop trying to find ways to show caring, compassion, and love when we need it most.*

48

# The Store-Brand Monologue

## Tuesday, November 22

Everyone is home!  Laughter tonight at the kitchen table…the kind that I only wish I could bottle for the quiet days.  My son made French toast and sausage for all.  The best story of today:

My son:  (unhappy) Don't buy store brand syrup.
Me:  (defensively) I didn't.
My son:  (sounding disgusted) I did.
*Laughter then silence.*
Me:  Why?
My son:  I don't know.  Dad was with me.
*More laughter.*
My son:  (looking distraught) And, the worst part, the worst part is I bought *two*, because they were two for three dollars.  It's like the Pop-Tarts, Mom told me not to buy the store brand Pop-Tarts.  I bought the store brand Pop-Tarts.  *Sigh.*

Yes, my dear son, you, and your store brand monologue are the star of this story.  These are the moments I missed so very much last year when I was sick and resting on the couch.  I vividly remember feeling almost like an outsider in my own home…no energy to cherish and appreciate this small stuff.

*The wisdom in this story:  I forgot how good it feels to laugh. A little more wisdom — never buy the store brand peanut butter either.*

# *Feeling Thankful*

**Sunday, November 27**

I have learned what is truly important. For years, my husband and I ate two big meals on every major holiday: Thanksgiving, Christmas, and Easter. My mom wanted us at home with her for the holidays, and of course my husband's mom wanted us home with her. My husband ate large portions both places, and smiled pleasantly. I didn't really enjoy my meal at either place, as I wanted to take enough to be polite but ended up eating a lot at one house and nothing at the other. I vividly recall a Christmas season when my mother was very unhappy with me. My husband and I were dating but not yet engaged, and my grandmother had traveled a great distance to be with us. While she sat in the kitchen fretting over my absence, I was spending time with someone else's grandparents. At the time, my eighteen-year-old self didn't realize how hurtful my not being there was to my own grandmother. Sadly, my grandmother passed away just a few years later. One might think a lesson would have been learned after that dreadful Christmas, but nope — we continued to try to split our time (and our portions) between two homes. On many holidays, I was absent from my own mother's dinner table to be with my husband's family. I deeply regret this, as I come from a small family. When I didn't come home, my parents' house felt empty. My husband has a large family, so my absence there would have been less noted. This year, we ate Thanksgiving Day dinner with my husband's family. My family planned to celebrate on a different day, because to us, Thanksgiving is truly every day. My sister and her family will be here soon, the turkey is in the oven and we will count our blessings.

**The wisdom in this story: Together is what matters, no matter the day.**

# *Get Yourself a Damn 5-Gallon Bucket*

## Thursday, December 1

My mother had a cousin who called her "Punk." It was an affectionate nickname, and sadly I don't remember the story of how it ever came to be. I think it started sweetly as Punkin' and over the years evolved into Punk. As children, they grew up as neighbors, and he once threatened to throw her beloved dog Peaches in the outhouse. As she ran to tell his mother, the story was he was going to throw peaches…and it took awhile for my great-aunt to realize that she meant Peaches the dog, not *peaches*. My mother was distraught, but laughed in telling the story years later. I remember this cousin well, and all of my childhood visits to mom's hometown included a visit to see him and his family. He had three children…a son too old to acknowledge me, a daughter who was my sister's age, and a son my age who once threatened to push me down their big hill of a driveway on his bike. I was secretly a little afraid of the cousin my age (and yet years later laugh about the "push you down the driveway" story); but the fun in visiting my older cousin made up for it. He loved beer, his language was colorful, and he was just plain fun. There was always a laugh when he was around. He called me Mich *(Mish)*. He is the only one in my life who has ever called me Mich. His wife is simply dear, she loves to shop and bake and *always* offered me candy when we visited. When I was married and living a life of my own, my visits to the western part of the state where they live became infrequent. My grandmother had since passed away, and even my mother didn't travel to that part of the state often. I shouldn't have been surprised, *he was loyal*, to see him at my mother's funeral. Oh, how he loved her. He put his arm around my shoulder and simply held me tightly. This big tough strong man had tears in his eyes when he reminisced about their childhood together. We promised to stay in touch, but life gets busy, and I didn't honestly know when our paths would cross again. When my kids were small, a family vacation in the area had us just passing through briefly. My son *loved* my cousin, (for the same reasons I always did) and always called him "the funny one." Although our visits weren't often, my daughters' cheerleading competitions and dairy events in recent years led us to the western part of the state, and we always stopped for a visit. My cousin had struggled with his own health (colon cancer, just like my mom), and was often napping in his favorite recliner chair when we arrived. He no longer had beer on the back porch, but rather bruises on his arms that he claimed were from carrying groceries. Inside of him, cancer raged…somewhat unbeknownst to him, and perhaps even with a bit of denial on his part. I visited him shortly after I was diagnosed and the curse words came out full force. He proceeded to tell me how awful chemo was for him, how much he hated his medi-ports, and found just about every colorful word he could to describe what I now know as my worst awful. However, he was careful to follow it up with "You'll be fine, we're made of good stuff! We're McDowell's! get yourself a damn 5-gallon bucket, and keep it right here by your side. That chemo shit will make you throw up." Shortly after that visit, I returned home and started chemo. I recall one occasion I was in the bathroom and *(too much information)* things were coming out at both ends. I realized I had never gotten myself a damn 5-gallon bucket, and I cursed myself for not listening to my cousin. I had a total of four chemo treatments, every 21-days, and my dear cousin called me to check in—*every single time.* It meant the world to me. When I thanked him for calling, he said, "Why wouldn't I, we're family." My last visit with him was in June, after I had completed treatments. I didn't stay long, but long enough to laugh at him cursing at his wife's dog, and making fun of her small-size SUV, which he called "a half a car." He loved to tell stories and on my way out of town, I decided to drive past the old homestead, where he and my mother had experienced life on the farm. The roads seemed unfamiliar to me *(damn chemo brain)* and I was at the far of edges of town before I realized I was lost. I called him, describing my whereabouts, and he asked, "What the hell road did you take? You're not even close to where you are supposed to be." He laughed out loud to know that I was lost, and guided me back on the right path, but not without me laughing until it was hard to catch my breath. As I took a walk down my mom's memory lane, I smiled knowing she would be glad he and I had kept in touch. She would be glad to know he cared enough to call when I was sick, but after all, why wouldn't he—we're family. As I drove out of town, I asked my daughter to sketch a brief map of landmarks that would help me find my way around "next time." I didn't realize that "next time" would be for my cousin's funeral. Just today, I was at my desk after school, and my cell phone rang...with a very familiar number. I answered quickly, expecting to hear his cheerful voice. It was his wife's friend. My cousin passed away yesterday, after a week in the hospital and a call to Hospice. I didn't ask for the medical details, but prayed the service wouldn't be on a weekday. *(Last year's illness exhausted my sick days and I am careful to keep the few I earned this year for my frequent follow-up appointments).* Saturday—the service would be on Saturday. *There is absolutely no doubt in my mind, I will be there. Why wouldn't I—we're family.* I'm still at school, typing this story furiously into my laptop as the tears flow endlessly. My tears surprise me a bit. How many times have I seen this man in the last thirty years? Ten, maybe fewer, but family is family— through thick and through thin—and through cancer. Saturday will be a hard day for me. Cancer sucks. My cousin turned 80 this year. He lived a great life, but I suspect he wasn't quite done living yet. My cousin had a strong faith, and gave me the words to a hymn that he said helped keep him strong on his hardest days. I wish I knew the tune. The title is enough to help me remember him with a smile:

*One Day at a Time, Sweet Jesus*
*by Marijohn Wilkin*

*I'm only human; I'm just a man.*
*Help me believe in what I could be*
*And all that I am*
*Show me the stairway I have to climb*
*Lord for my sake, help me to take*
*One day at a time*

*One day at a time sweet Jesus*
*That's all I'm askin' of you*
*Just give me the strength*
*To do every day what I have to do*
*Yesterday's gone sweet Jesus*
*And tomorrow may never be mine*
*Lord, help me today, show me the way*
*One day at a time*

**The wisdom in this story: Cousins are your first friends, and they will love you forever...even if they try to throw Peaches in the outhouse and make you cry when you are six.**

# No, I'm Not Pregnant

**Friday, December 2**

It started a few days ago, in the middle of a sleepless night. I started to wonder why I can't shake the tired. I didn't want to believe it was my body trying to recover from a turbulent year. I didn't want to believe it was a side effect from my medication. I didn't want to believe that night after night of sleeplessness makes it difficult to shake the tired. I wanted an answer. I had noticed the weight gain. I didn't want to believe it was my body's reaction to eating normal foods after chemo nausea and little to eat. I didn't want to believe it was a side effect from my medication. I didn't want to believe that day after day of the drive-thru donut shop makes one gain weight. I wanted an answer. I started to wonder why I've been a little extra emotional lately. I didn't want to believe it was hormonal, not uncommon in women my age. I didn't want to believe it was a side effect from my medication. I didn't want to believe that in simple words, cancer and the fear of recurrence will always be a part of my story. I wanted an answer. My mind began to wander back to my July gynecology appointment when the doctor told me that two different samples of bloodwork confirmed that I was most definitely post-menopause. No need for contraception. When I asked for one more blood draw just to be sure, *and remember, I'm the one who hates needles*...he looked a little annoyed, told me it wasn't necessary, but handed me the order to have blood drawn. "Wait a couple of months," he said..."since you just had it done a few weeks ago." One September morning on my way to work I had blood drawn. The center was a little slower than I had anticipated and I realized I would be arriving to work late. I felt silly for insisting on just one more reassurance that I was post-menopause. Then came the phone call, "The doctor would like you to know that your ovaries are still kicking." *Seriously.* Is there not more of a professional way of saying such a thing? Not post-menopause. Anyway, I went about my day and didn't really think much more about that call until a few days ago. Tired. Weight gain. Emotional. Swollen breasts, *or was that more one-sided, swollen post-surgery breast-cancer-breast, singular?* I thought back to times in my younger years when tired, weight gain, emotional, and swollen breasts caused the rejoicing that comes with pregnancy. Oh. My. Goodness. *(Punctuation out of place, words sinking in...)* Could I possibly be pregnant? My husband and I had always wanted four children, and the three we have were conceived through the use of fertility drugs and careful planning. How could I possibly be pregnant without even trying? No, not possible. Go to sleep, Michele. Then the thoughts returned to me in daytime hours. What if? In my mind, I had a conversation with my practically grown children; rehearsing what I would say to them about assuming responsibility for this potential little one should my cancer return or my husband and I be simply too old to properly parent. I had to tell myself to refocus, for my thoughts were getting way too far ahead of me. As I took my nighttime medication, the one that some cancer patients take for five years post-treatment, I noticed the warning label. *Do not take if you are pregnant or planning to become pregnant.* Sheer panic. What could my dosage of cancer drugs, routine ibuprofen use for joint pain, and lack of a good pre-natal vitamin do to a developing fetus? Stop. Pull yourself together, Michele, you are seriously starting to sound like a crazy person. I knew I needed an answer...the kind of answer that comes from a little pee-on-the-stick type pregnancy test. *A pregnancy test.* I hadn't bought one in nearly sixteen years. I didn't think I could buy a pregnancy test. What if someone would see me? What would they think? Would they think I was seriously pregnant at my age? Then I thought of my children. Oh, no! If people saw me buying a pregnancy test, they might think one of my teenage daughters is pregnant. Or would they even consider that I could be buying one for my son's sweet girlfriend? No, I could not buy a pregnancy test. I casually asked my husband who was planning to run some errands if he would mind picking up a pregnancy test. I think he thinks I'm nuts. He smiled the gentle smile I've always loved; chuckled a little, and said "I really don't think you're pregnant." He came home with a pregnancy test. He bought the name brand...a two-pack. I married a good man. My husband has surely noticed the tired, heavier, emotional me, and he probably wants answers, too. It's 2AM; I just peed on the stick. Alone in the bathroom, trying not to make any noises that would wake the dogs that would wake the kids, I peed on the stick. It was much different than years ago, when my husband and I both hovered over the stick waiting for that elusive second blue line to appear. My husband, snoring in our bed, probably thought I would wait until morning to do the test. At my age, the bladder can't wait until morning. I watched and waited the full three minutes. One single blue line. Not pregnant. My mind was awhirl. Relief, but I suppose also a little bit of sadness. I am smart enough to know that a pregnancy at my age and after all my body has been through this past year would never be a good idea. But somewhere, a little part of me never gave up hope on that fourth child. I crawled into bed and didn't even realize I was crying until my college-age daughter's dog (who just happens to sleep on my pillow while she is at school) licked my cheek. I am tired because a dog sleeps on my pillow. I am obese for many reasons, but the frequent donuts don't help with the weight-loss. I am emotional because I am somewhere in the throes of menopause, and I just had one hell of a year fighting cancer. But I am not pregnant. I am an insane insomniac and I need to go to sleep. In the morning I will pee on the second stick, *just to be sure,* and I will stop at the donut shop on my way to work. Next week, I will do my best to eat healthier, let my mind wander less, and recognize that I have every right to be emotional.

*The wisdom in this story: It never really occurred to me what people might think if they saw my husband buying a pregnancy test. No, he is not having a mid-life crisis affair with a pregnant mistress. He is right here by my side wondering why I never sleep, and holding my hand in my moments of insanity.*

# "Why would you tell?"

## Wednesday, December 7

I was invited by a local retailer to sell my book at their "Ladies' Night." A large area of the store hosted vendors of every product imaginable. Women young and old alike, visited to shop their hearts out buying from home businesses — kitchen items, home décor, tote bags, makeup, handmade jewelry, and even clothing. This retailer had generously decided to donate their raffle and door prize proceeds for breast cancer research. They invited me to sit at the front of the store and greet the guests as they arrived. While my book display was pretty and inviting, those women had one thing on their minds — *door prizes and raffles*. Where do we enter? Do we have to be here to win? No, these ladies weren't here to chat with me and buy a book; they were here for the prizes! Near the end of the evening, two ladies came to the table to ask about the grand prize. They asked me if I sold many books. I replied that I hadn't and added, "It's kind of a hard sell. A cancer story — needs a pretty specific audience." One lady whispered, "I understand," and pointed toward the other lady. She then quietly said, "My sister was just diagnosed." I glanced at the sister, hoping to offer encouraging words. She was glaring at her sister and said, "Why would you tell?" Then silence. It was most definitely an awkward moment. The sister who wanted to share meant well, and certainly did not intend to betray a confidence. However, it wasn't her story to tell. I suspect they both have a long road ahead of them, one as patient the other as caregiver. I scribbled a quick message inside of a book and handed it to her, whispering "my gift to you." I suppose it was ample compensation in case they didn't win a door prize.

*The wisdom in this story: Respect the privacy of others.*

# What a Difference a Year Makes

### Saturday, December 10

Despite the chilly air, I was awake, showered, and dressed early today. I paused to reflect on the stillness around me, the slightest snoring from the dog at the foot of my bed in an otherwise quiet house. My youngest daughter will be awake soon, as today is her aerial yoga day. While she is twisting her flexible body into many challenging yoga poses, I will sit and listen to the calming voice of her instructor. The soft background music will make me feel incredibly relaxed, somewhat sleepy even. The light fragrance of aromatherapy oil will envelop the room and I will decide the yoga studio is one of my happy places. Oh how I wish my tired, crippled body could twist in the fancy yoga formations. However, for today it is simply a joy to be alive. After yoga, I will be returning to my favorite salon for a haircut, feeling thankful that my hair has finally grown long enough to style.

*The wisdom in this story: I am finding joy in the simple things.*

# *My Heart is Happy*

**Friday, December 16**

My oldest daughter just finished her first semester of freshman year of college; she is home. All of my children are under the same roof again, even if only for a little while.

*The wisdom in this story: Even though I know they must sometimes roam, I'm happiest when they're all at home.*

# *Somewhere in my Memory*

**Tuesday, December 20**

"Candles in the window,
shadows painting the ceiling,
gazing at the fire glow,
feeling that gingerbread feeling.

Precious moments,
special people,
happy faces,
I can see.

Somewhere in my memory,
Christmas joys all around me,
living in my memory,
all of the music,
all of the magic,
all of the family,
home here with me.

*Music written by John Williams*
*Lyrics written by Leslie Bricusse*

**The wisdom in this story:  Christmas joys are all around me.**

# *Christmas Day Courage*

## Sunday, December 25

With all of the hustle and bustle of the holiday, Christmas morning snuck up on me this year. I awoke early, even before my children. While I spent some quiet time reflecting, it occurred to me that at this time last year, I had the courage to ask my son to clipper cut my hair. When I think back to my hair loss, clipper cut, razor cut, and the baldness that ensued…my choice to cut my hair before it all fell out was a courageous one. I wouldn't have wanted to do it any other way.

*The wisdom in this story: I was braver than I believed, stronger than I seemed, and loved more than I knew.*

# *That's Why We See You*

## Wednesday, December 28

Today was a follow-up appointment with the oncologist. I thought I would be fine. Then, I walked into the waiting room. The people in the waiting room tug at your heartstrings. Sickness. Sadness. Heartache. Cancer sucks. My tears started as soon as the doctor walked into the room. I told her I was worried about my emotions. I told her I feel frustrated. I have lost my ability to multi-task, and my energy levels have not yet returned to what I had hoped. I told her I'm angry about cancer, and cry when I hear of a friend or loved one newly diagnosed. I told her that compassion can be a wonderful thing, but I was a little worried about myself. I told her I'm struggling—something that is hard for me to admit. She smiled a warm, reassuring smile and said this:

> *"You're not being patient enough with yourself.*
> *We hit you with some really harsh drugs.*
> *Your body needs some time to recover.*
> *Give it some time – two years."*

I don't believe I am depressed—*pissed* may be a more appropriate word. Cancer interrupted my life. Cancer took me on a path through some of my darkest days. Cancer had the potential to rip a family apart, but we said, "*Screw you cancer*" and held on tightly to one another. I feel blessed that my story had a happy ending; as for some people cancer steals lives. I am happy, living life to the fullest, and appreciating my good health, but the thought of cancer fills my mind every single day. I need to work on being patient. I thanked the doctor for taking the time to listen to my concerns. She smiled a knowing smile, and simply said, "That's why we see you."

**The wisdom in this story: "Patience is a virtue."**

# *Happy New Year*

## Sunday, January 1

I love there are cards for every occasion even though I seldom send them.  While to me it seems silly sending a New Year's card, I loved the sentiment in this one I saw recently:

> *Wishing you beautiful moments,*
> *treasured memories*
> *and all the blessings a heart can know.*

Wow!  That so beautifully sums up my prayer for each day!

*The wisdom in this story:  Every New Year truly is worth celebrating.  Maybe next year I'll start sending cards!*

# *My Why*

**Wednesday, January 4**

Today I started a new weight loss program. The program offers participants a meal-tracking system, a weigh-in opportunity, and a support group type meeting. This is the third time in my adult life I have joined, and they say the third time is a charm, so maybe I will lose the weight and begin to feel healthier. As I sat through the meeting, my eyes scanned the members. Some were thin—obviously people who had met their goal weight and still attended for accountability. Some appeared to have a lot of weight to lose, as much as I do, even more. Others appeared tired and worn. I couldn't help but wonder if it was from frustrations with obesity, harder lifestyles, or if some had even traveled the same cancer path as mine. While I wondered why people were there, I suppose they wondered the same thing about me. At the end of the meeting, new-members gathered for clarification about the program and time for questions and answers. We were encouraged to write in our journals our "why"—why were we there? What helped us to make the decision to start this path to weight-loss? Some people looked lost in thought, but I knew immediately what to write…

*I fought too hard to live.*

Yes, last year I faced the hardest fight I've ever known. I came out on the other side still smiling. I cannot, and will not, let obesity *(and my obsession with donuts)* be the reason for continued health problems. We were given an opportunity to share our "why" and I shared mine. It felt good to have a common goal with these people who just an hour ago were complete strangers.

**The wisdom in this story: One day at a time, one pound at a time, I can do this—because I fought too hard to live.**

# *My Kind of Friend*

## Wednesday, January 11

I am the only one who could possibly attend a weight-loss center meeting and make a new friend who would invite me *to dinner.* Seriously. I'm going to these meetings to try to eat healthier, or rather eat in moderation—one donut instead of five. While I love the support, I almost found it laugh out loud funny that one of the sweet ladies there invited me to join her and two others for dinner…*"and we REALLY eat," she had whispered.* I declined for this evening, but I also recognize how important it is to treat myself once in awhile. She said they go to a different restaurant each week. As soon as I reach my first ten-pound weight loss, I'm going to join them. I think I'll bring donuts for dessert.

*The wisdom in this story: My current weight loss program is points-based. My daily point allowance is 38. One chocolate frosted donut is 12 points.*

# *Gone Too Soon*

## Thursday, January 19

My oldest daughter is still home from college. While her friends who attend other colleges returned weeks ago, her school's winter break doesn't end for a few more days. I love having her home, but I think she is ready to go back. My husband playfully suggested she forget college altogether and we hire her permanently as our housekeeper and chef. She is simply amazing. She thinks returning to college and pursuing a career in education sounds like a better option, and I can't really blame her. Aside from running errands for me, she spends her days at home. Home alone with three dogs. I did that last year, it gets lonely. My daughter has cleaned, organized, and cooked for us daily. Most recently, she decided to clean out her bedroom closet. The top shelf contained items I considered treasures, for which this college girl now has no space. As always when my children find things they no longer need, they place them in *my* bedroom. For, I am the sentimental one, the one who has trouble parting with things. While I can never turn the clock back to when my children were small, certain things bring the warmest of reminders. When I entered my room, I was surprised at just how much my daughter had placed there. There was the Winnie the Pooh jewelry box that held her very first bracelet, a gift she received on her first birthday. There was the sleeping bag she used as a young child, which immediately reminded me of her first sleepover parties away from home. There was the small travel bag we once called her first suitcase. There was another box, painstakingly covered with one hundred pom-pom balls — an elementary school project for the 100th Day of School. There was the oscillating fan purchased for cheerleading camp, her first far-away-from-home experience. All of these moments, stacked in neat piles on the wicker trunk at the foot of my bed. I started to cry. At first, I believe

I was mourning the fact that my daughter no longer had a need for these things. Then, I realized I was crying for a different reason. I was crying because I was so blessed to have experienced all of these wonderful "mom moments" — the joy of celebrating a Winnie-the-Pooh themed first birthday; the joy of seeing her have trusted friends to laugh and giggle with in the middle of the night; the joy of seeing her pack a suitcase and yearn to travel; the joy of counting school days, all while knowing they pass too quickly even without counting; and the joy of sending this child far from home, knowing even when there are tears, I am still able to soothe her. Bits and pieces of eighteen years of this sweet girl's life, placed before me, and I cried more. Again, I was crying for a different reason. I thought of the young mother from my church who was diagnosed with breast cancer when our children were just toddlers. Her wish was to live to see her daughter start Kindergarten. Sadly, she passed away in August, just before our girls started Kindergarten. She was 39. I thought of my high school classmate, whose children attend school with mine. She, too, had breast cancer. She didn't live long enough to see all of the 100th Day of School projects, or to see her children start high school. She died when her oldest child was in middle school. She was 43. I think of another special mom dear to my heart, who died when her daughter was just sweet sixteen. She didn't live long enough to be here for her daughter's senior prom or high school graduation. Then, I thought of the mothers who are weeping because they have lost a child to cancer. Yes, I have been so very blessed.

*The wisdom in this story: My friends whose kids went back to college weeks ago tell me that they are gone too soon. But for me, gone too soon has a whole different meaning.*

# *A Rose Gold Reminder*

## Thursday, February 2

Fourteen months ago today, I gifted each of my first grade students with a silicone wristband embossed with the words HOPE, STRENGTH, and LOVE. I explained:

> *These pink wristbands say HOPE because we hope that someday there will be no cancer in the world.*

> *These pink wristbands say STRENGTH because you help me to be strong as I fight the cancer.*

> *These pink wristbands say LOVE because it is always important to tell someone you love them. Sometimes cancer reminds us to say, "I love you."*

At the same time, I slipped one of the wristbands onto my own wrist. I have worn that wristband every single day since. On some of my darkest days, the words reminded me I could never give up hope. The words reminded me I needed to be strong. Most importantly, the words reminded me to say I love you...as much as possible...to friends and family who wrapped me in their love. In October, I added a second wristband, imprinted with a butterfly and the sentiment *Living Beyond Breast Cancer.* I had hoped the addition of the second wristband would remind me the worst of my journey is over, and I am well on my way to healing. However, it wasn't quite so magical. The words breast cancer started to fade from the wristband, and I realized imprinted wristbands aren't really as nice as embossed ones. I learned while the worst of my journey is over, and I am well on my way to healing, cancer will always be a part of my story. I live with small side effects and regular reminders daily. I removed the *Living Beyond Breast Cancer* wristband and gently slid a shiny new rose gold and silver watch onto my arm. This rose gold and silver watch would serve as a new reminder. As I watched the second hand tick so rhythmically past the roman numerals, I couldn't help but smile.  It looks very pretty, and nicely matches a wristband I'm not quite ready to remove — the one so beautifully embossed with the words HOPE, STRENGTH, and LOVE.

***The wisdom in this story:  None of us really know how much time we have, and we should cherish every single second of every single day.***

p.s.  My husband surprised me with a beautiful rose gold, silver, and diamond ring for my birthday/Valentine's Day.  I had never really talked with him about this new significance of rose gold.  He knows me well…

# Spa Visit with My Sister

## Sunday, February 5

When I took my daughter to a local spa for a day of pampering for her 18th birthday, she innocently asked, "Why don't we celebrate *your* birthday here?" The answer was fairly simple. It was expensive—an indulgence even. I don't spend much money on myself, and would never have felt deserving of such a treat on my own. We had a wonderful day, and decided a spa visit would become a regular occurrence on each of our birthdays. My birthday is tomorrow. In scheduling our chocolate pedicures, I decided I couldn't indulge without inviting my youngest daughter, too. So, I made a reservation for not one, not two, but three of us! It was most definitely a stretch for our finances, but a day I knew we would cherish. Last night, my youngest daughter complained of a sore throat. A quick trip to the urgent care center confirmed it was strep. No spa for the strep girl, sigh. To say she was disappointed would be an understatement. She felt certain she could take her antibiotics and go along. I felt certain there is a guideline I have followed since before she was born that one must be taking an antibiotic for 24-hours before they are no longer contagious. She pleaded, and I stood firm in my decision. I was not taking strep girl to the spa. The spa cancellation policy was 24 hours, and I had missed that window of time. I would lose my money if I didn't find someone to go in her place. The first person who came to mind was my sister. When I invited her, she responded with an enthusiastic *"Yes!"* When we picked her up this morning, we chuckled to see that she carried a large bag. She looked like she had packed for an overnighter! When we explained there are lockers, bathrobes, flip flops, and a locker room with chocolate shampoos, conditioners, and body wash at the spa, she asked what we were taking in with us. Our answer was simple, "A book to read." Yes, this was a day of indulgence, something that became more evident by the minute my sister had never experienced. I thought about our mother — who did little to pamper herself. My mother loved her lipstick, but didn't fuss much about other pampering. The only time I can really recall my mother wearing nail polish was when the Hospice nurses used to polish her toes. I felt a tear trickle down my cheek and wished more than anything my mother could have a spa day, too. However, today was a happy day and I was going to soak in the sweet scents and tastes of chocolate and pamper myself. While I missed having my younger daughter along, I was glad my sister could have this experience in her place. As we sat by the fireplace in the quiet room, both my sister and daughter were deeply engrossed in reading their books. Me? I was eating chocolate and counting my blessings. The joy of this moment distracted me even of the simple task of reading.

*The wisdom in this story: Everyone deserves a spa day.*

# *Strawberries, Roses, and a Toilet Plunger*

## Tuesday, February 14

I have always hated the commercialism of Valentine's Day. Years ago, I told my husband I would much rather he send me flowers at different times throughout the year, than pay double the price for a red-rose bouquet on Valentine's Day. I'm much more of a white-daisy kind of girl anyway. However, those different times throughout the year don't really happen, and I find myself feeling a bit wistful and even melancholy on most Valentine's Days. My co-workers have husbands who send flowers to school, and as showy as it seems, I sometimes think I would like that a bit. But that makes it seem like the flowers are more for show than "just because," and then I go right back to hating the obnoxious commercialism of the day. Social media is also an outlet where many of my friends love to post pictures of gifts received, and declare their love to their spouses. My husband doesn't use social media, so if I declared my love for him there, it would be more for show than "just because." He wouldn't even see it! Now, just a few weeks ago, my husband did surprise me with a beautiful rose gold, silver, and diamond ring for my birthday/Valentine's Day combined. I thought I was going to cry when I opened it, and so instead, I scolded him a bit and said, "How much did it cost? We don't spend money like this—" My son told me to stop acting like "all girls" and saying he shouldn't have gotten me anything, when I really knew deep down that I wanted something and was appreciative. He said, "Mom, just accept it and say thank you." My son is wise beyond his years. So, I accepted it and said thank you. My husband found himself "off the hook" for two occasions and knew that I wouldn't be silently sulking on either my birthday or Valentine's Day. It didn't mean I wouldn't be looking at and analyzing what every other couple I knew did on that day reserved for sweethearts. Not surprisingly, I was too busy to visit the main office on Valentine's Day, so I have no knowledge of the flower deliveries made to my school. Social media that evening, however, was a different story. Some of the entries seemed to over-dramatize relationships, and made me question whether or not these couples are as deliriously happy as they want others to think. Some of the posts included,

*"Love to my one and only Valentine for 30+ years…"*

*"I'm sending my wife love songs from the decades."*

*"I love you." (followed by the spouse posting of "I love you more.")*

*I made a nice meal at home. Dinner was good, dessert even better."*
(um, that comment made me blush a little, as this particular couple often makes sexual comments publicly…or was my own mind wandering between the lines?)

Then there was my sister's post. Hers was a collage photo, and included four photos — a plate of gourmet chocolate dipped strawberries, a beautiful vase arrangement of fresh red roses, a red and gold-tone embossed greeting card, and a toilet plunger…yes, a *toilet plunger*. Her message was simply stated:

*"Happy Valentine's Day! Last night my kitchen was filled with the smell of chocolate strawberries and the sound of my children laughing. I spent today surrounded by a caring group of second graders followed by beautiful roses and a card from my husband. My day would not have been complete without having to plunge the toilet. I always said that changing diapers was the easy part of parenting. As sweet as they have grown up to be…they will always be full of crap. I love them anyway."*

There, on the most popular of social media pages, my sister shared her wisdom. As much as strawberries, roses, cards, and laughter make us all smile and sometimes the envy of others — the toilet plunger is the reality of life. In my journey throughout the past year and a half, there have been many sunny days, but also a lot of days that were simply crap. On those days, I relied on my sister's best wisdom: "one day at a time."

**The wisdom in this story: The toilet plunger is the reality of life.**

# *Missing Mom*

**Wednesday, February 22**

Today would have been my mother's 82nd birthday. I can't imagine her as an 82 year old, as cancer stole her away when she was only 66. I like to think if my mom were still living, she would be an old woman who always wears purple. I like to think she would regularly go for coffee with friends, although only one of her three best friends is still living. I like to think she would find great joy in her grandchildren, as they have grown up to be wonderful young adults. I like to think she and I would never run out of things to talk about and we would sit together on the couch and laugh until we cry. People say that time heals all wounds, and the sadness of missing someone dissipates over time. I disagree. My mom was an incredibly special lady, and I still miss her every single day. I like to believe my mother is in Heaven, a beautiful place high above the clouds. I like to believe angels of all ages wear purple. I like to believe my mother has been reunited with her lost friends and loved ones and there is an endless supply of coffee in Heaven. I like to think my mother is watching us all from above and keeping a close careful eye on her grandchildren. I like to think when my own children and I sit on the couch and our conversations turn into explosive laughter my mother has something to do with it.

*The wisdom in this story: Today should have been so different. I'm celebrating Mom on this side of Heaven.*

# *Passed Away Unexpectedly*

## Wednesday, March 1

Today I received news that a dear friend passed away unexpectedly. We first met when our boys started Kindergarten...sixteen years of friendship. She had a son and two daughters, and I have the same. In many ways, our lives paralleled one another. My earliest memories of her include cheering for our children on the soccer sidelines in rain and sunshine...*more rain than sunshine.* Together, we attended PTO meetings and events where we both served on what seemed like one-too-many committees. There were playdates and birthday parties, and countless pictures of smiling kids and birthday cakes. I was once the Girl Scout leader for our daughters, and she stood by her son as he worked through the ranks of Eagle Scout. We attended elementary school holiday parties and worked booths at the spring fairs. At middle school concerts we applauded until our hands ached. As the years passed, there were Varsity football games under the Friday night lights, and football dinners in our homes for the seniors. Years and years of memories, but perhaps my favorite memory of this special friend was of our carpool days. When our boys played midget football, our daughters attended a gymnastics class...*in the opposite direction on the map.* We met at the end of my driveway on a regular basis. One of us drove the boys to the football field, while the other drove the girls to the gym. We didn't always plan ahead, and found joy in whichever route we happened to take each evening. I remember our daughters being very quiet, and I tried to make conversation or play the radio to ease the pain of the silence. The boys, while quiet in their own way, seemed to forget I was in the car with them. It was on those rides where I heard them call one another "dude" and "man" and discuss which middle school teachers they liked, *and disliked.* Occasionally, but not often, the conversation turned to girls.

In what seemed like the blink of an eye, I watched these little "dudes" turn into grown men, and I couldn't have been more proud of them. At a time when many others were turning to drugs and alcohol, "our boys" had jobs, spent time with family, and enjoyed going hunting and fishing with their dads. We often talked about how very blessed we were to have such terrific kids...daughters included. As our kids became more independent, my friend and I still made time to meet for an occasional lunch date. Looking back, we never made *enough* time. Last July, my friend called me. She was *very* concerned about how I was doing. I assured her that I had completed my treatments and I was doing well...energy levels slowly starting to return. We made plans for a lunch date the next day. Something came up, and she couldn't make it. We promised to reschedule. August came, then back to school and life got busy...*really busy*. We hadn't talked since, but that isn't really unusual for a friendship that spans over many years. It always seemed like we were able to pick up right where we left off each time we met. I can't even begin to explain the sadness I felt when I read the news of her passing in an e-mail from a neighbor. The neighbor who sent the e-mail was once instrumental in our PTO and seeing her name brought back a flood of elementary school memories. This time, the details were very simple and matter of fact...our dear friend had passed away unexpectedly, husband found her dead, making arrangements, very sad news, heart aches for the children, will let you know the specifics of the service. She signed her e-mail *"With great sadness,"* which made me cry even more. As tears fell from my eyes, I realized nothing could have prepared me for this news. Knowing the days ahead will be difficult ones, I try to find comfort in my memories. I tried to remember how my dear friend and I ended our last phone conversation. Sadly, I don't remember.

**The wisdom in this story: "Never pass a chance to say I love you, because we aren't promised tomorrow." (unknown)**

# *The Kindergarten Boys*

## Thursday, March 2

The obituary announced a visitation at the funeral home on Thursday, and a service to follow on Friday. While the initial shock of yesterday's e-mail had worn off, it was all still a bit surreal. I felt numb. It didn't seem possible that my friend of sixteen years was gone — gone too soon. My husband, son, and I traveled to the funeral home together for the visitation. Upon parking the car, I was overcome with emotion. I couldn't get out of the car. I remember telling myself, *"just breathe,"* but every time I tried to take a deep breath I just shuddered silently and the tears flowed even more. A quick drink of water seemed to calm me, and I apologized for my emotion. I told my son, "I'm not very good at these things." I reminded him, "This isn't easy, but it's something in life that you have to do for others." He responded quietly, "I *know* Mom, that's why I'm here." *I wondered what must have been going through his mind — to watch me fight so hard to live last year, and to now to see his friend's mom pass away so unexpectedly.* As I walked through the doors of the funeral home, with two strong men at my side, I thought I was okay. Then came time to sign the guest register. We were early to arrive, and only around fifteen to twenty people had already registered their attendance. My eyes quickly scanned the list. The first two names stood out to me immediately…Michael and Robert… two boys (now young men) who had also attended Kindergarten with my son. Simply seeing their names caused me to cry again, at which moment I politely excused myself and stood by a beautiful fireplace in the newly built funeral home. I held onto the mantle to steady myself, and tried not to blink, because I knew if I did a flood of tears would come. A few deep breaths later, I quietly announced that I was ready to go inside the room where the visitation was being held. Following my family's lead, I entered the room, albeit

79

reluctantly. I gazed at the flowers, praying that the pungent floral aroma didn't make me nauseous as it did at my own mother's funeral. The flowers looked delicate and perfect. A water droplet glistened on one of the red roses, and I couldn't help but notice that the whole arrangement was red and white...the colors of our football team. *Focus, Michele, focus...breathe, Michele, breathe.* I was okay until my friend's husband made eye contact with me. As I looked into his eyes, I saw a depth of sadness I had never seen before. My heart hurt. This tall, brave man who had seen his family endure other trials and heartaches, now dealing with something he described as simply unreal. *The kids...oh how could I possibly look at the kids?* There they were in age order, and I wondered for a brief moment if someone had planned it that way, or if they all just sort of fell into place. Their son, the oldest, hugged me tightly and firmly accepted my handshake and offer of condolences. The middle daughter was the one I knew the least of the three, and she was next in line. She also reached out to accept my warm embrace, and I wondered what it must be like for such quiet, shy children to have to endure the hugs of strangers. Next was the youngest daughter. While she and my daughter still attend school together, it is a large school, and their paths don't cross often. I hadn't seen her in awhile...and she looked so very grown up. While there were tears in her eyes, she remained stoic. These kids were doing so well — my friend would have been proud of them. Just as I was ready to fall into a nearby chair, I spotted the Kindergarten Boys. As they were the first to arrive, I felt certain they would have already been gone by the time I got there. Not so — there they were: Michael, Robert, and some other classmates. My son had also joined the mix, and they all stood in somewhat awkward silence. Hugs were plentiful, and some of them whispered to me about shared memories of their growing up years. For a moment, it actually felt like time stood still. All of these sweet faces, gathered together to remember the life of someone so very dear. Slowly, the boys began to speak, but only slightly above a whisper, with knowing looks and glances of sadness. My thoughts turned to their Kindergarten teacher, and the whisper of a voice she often used in speaking to them. I could never remember a time when these otherwise rambunctious boys had been so quiet. It was a lovely testimony to the parents who raised them, and a clear show of respect for the solemn event they were attending. The Kindergarten Boys all gathered together after so many years, to show love, support, and compassion. Although most of them were age twenty-one, in my eyes they were still five years old. I should have been able to comfort them, but I discovered it was they who comforted me. Finally, I passed through their inner circle into the warm embrace of their parents. To say there wasn't a dry eye would be an understatement, and we all felt the same shock and sadness. I walked out the doors of the funeral home feeling the same sadness I did when I had entered, the sadness perhaps even intensified. I knew the funeral the next day would be even more difficult, but I knew it was something I had to do—for myself, for my friend, and for her husband and children. It has been said that when someone close to you dies unexpectedly, you may feel like you never got the chance to really say goodbye. I could only hope and pray that my friend knew how much she meant to me. While our kids grew up together, we also grew up together as parents. We celebrated the many milestones, and stressed over the humbling heartaches. What a life it had been for my friend—amidst the struggles, so many good, good memories. As my husband and I entered the funeral home hand in hand for the service the next day, I asked him why this seemed so much harder than all of the other services we have attended. His answer was simple…*"The kids."*

**The wisdom in this story: It's the things that you least expect that hit you the hardest.**

# *Gin and Tonic*

## Wednesday, March 8

I sound a little pathetic when I say I haven't gotten a good night's sleep since diagnosis, but that is the absolute truth. A variety of things keep me awake at night, including physical discomfort, fatigue (yes, there is such a thing as being *too* tired), newly noticed lumps and bumps that feel unusual, and more specifically, the never-ending fear of recurrence. While I am fortunate my cancer had not spread to lymph nodes *(meaning lesser chance of recurrence)*, once the word cancer enters your vocabulary, so does the fear. No matter what seems to go wrong in my life, physically or emotionally, I want to blame the cancer. Usually, it's in an angry muttering, *"damn cancer,"* but more often it comes in the form of tears. Last night was a tearful night for me. I seemed to toss and turn a bit more than usual, but it was more of a physical discomfort than what I experience on the nights when my mind is racing. I simply couldn't get comfortable. Just as I started to fall into a good sleep pattern, I awoke with excruciating cramps in my right leg. The cramping continued into my foot, and I leapt from the bed trying desperately to walk it out. Walking seemed to cause more pain, so I took a seat on my bathroom vanity stool where I proceeded to massage my calf and twist my foot back into what felt like a normal position. When the same cramping started in my left leg and foot, I started to panic. *What the hell is going on with me?* I've never been one to experience such leg cramps, and I eat a banana every single day to ensure that my body is getting adequate potassium. I drink large amounts of water each day to help with hydration and weight loss. So this pain — this unexplainable pain — it has to be related to *the cancer*. I was pretty sure this must be the pain some people complain about during and post chemo, but to experience it over a year after my last chemo treatment, puzzled me. I muttered "damn cancer" a bit more loudly than usual, and the tears started to flow. At this point, both legs and feet were cramping, and I didn't know which one to massage first. Through tears, I did what I had not needed to do in months — I desperately called my husband's name, and said, "I need help." *I need help.* This sucks. Cancer sucks. Chemo sucks. Leg cramps and not sleeping at night sucks. Once again, I felt defeated. My patient husband looked a bit bewildered, and massaged the pain from both legs before we retreated to the bedroom. He gently reminded me to "wake him any time," and I gently reminded myself that I married a good man. It took over an hour for the tears to go away, but the leg cramps didn't return. In the morning, I felt a bit of tightness, but nothing significant and most definitely not the cramping I had experienced during nighttime hours. Emotionally, I felt both sad and mad. I wanted answers, but it seems in a world of cancer, there really are no answers. I called my oncologist's office — voice mail, please leave a message. I hung up. Later, I called a second time. Voice mail, please leave a message. Teachers don't leave messages, because by the time someone calls you back, your moments free of teaching students have passed. Finally, I called a third time. The triage person who answered the phone seemed empathetic, and aware of reports of similar symptoms. After a quick, "I'm going to transfer you to a nurse" and a brief hold, a nurse answered. They never tell you if the first person shared your symptoms or not, so I repeated my story. As a patient, it seems anytime you have to tell a story twice it adds to the frustration. I asked, "Could it be the chemo so long ago? Could it be the estrogen receptor drug I currently take?" Before she could even answer, I think I knew what the answer was going to be. The answer came in a very dry form of "No, it's not the chemo. No, it's not the estrogen receptor drug. No, this isn't really related to the cancer." *(Although in my own mind — already made up — I knew it had to be...)* I asked if any bloodwork would be recommended to check levels, just in case the potassium had dipped as it had during chemotherapy treatments. "No, that would not be necessary." She told me my symptoms sounded like muscle spasms. She suggested I drink tonic water, and then giggled a bit when she told me it was my choice whether or not to add gin. Apparently, tonic water contains a natural form of quinine, a muscle relaxant. A quick online search tells me that the drug form of quinine is prescribed to treat malaria. It states that the drug is *not* recommended to treat or prevent nighttime leg cramps. I suppose in its natural form it must be acceptable. Another online search tells me that drinking alcohol with my currently prescribed estrogen receptor drug may cause side effects that include dizziness, drowsiness, and even increased risk for heart attacks and strokes. Hmm. While I knew the nurse's comment that it was my choice to add gin was sarcasm, what if someone didn't? Feeling frustrated, I failed to see the humor in anything — especially this nurse who obviously seemed to think I needed to drown my sorrows and spasms in alcohol. Being that she really offered me no sound explanation for anything, I surmised that maybe it is the cancer…maybe it is hormones…maybe; just maybe, it is simply a sign of getting older. For now, I will treat the symptoms as they come, waking my husband to help stretch my legs and dry my tears.

*The wisdom in this story: I think I need a gin and tonic.*

# *We are Complete*

**Friday, March 10**

My college girl is home. All five of us went out to dinner tonight, something that doesn't seem to happen so much lately. There were so many smiles and giggles! My kids are at the age where they make fun of their parents; and they find great joy in laughing when my words don't always come out right, *(yep, chemo brain)*. Although, it seems my husband sometimes has those moments, too — so maybe it truly is more aging than chemo that affects us. Either way, the kids find it terribly humorous, and once one of them starts laughing they all do. As we traveled home, and laughter ensued, my middle (college) daughter asked, "Is it this funny when I'm not around?" There was a resounding "No!" from the other kids, and my answer was simple. "When you are home, we are complete."

*The wisdom in this story: "To have all my dear ones together under one roof — that is all I ask of life." (D.E. Stevenson)*

# The Waiting Room

**Thursday, March 30**

Well, I'm thankful I was blessed with patience (and a fairly decent book to read). Due to a scheduling mix up (they scheduled me for a *screening* mammogram instead of a *diagnostic* mammogram), they were unable to do my mammogram today. So one pink gown, another long wait in the waiting room, and a few laughs later my mammogram is now scheduled for Monday.

*The wisdom in this story: One day at a time...*

# *Yams*

**Friday, March 31**

Spring is such an exciting time in a first grade classroom. In science, we are learning about plants, and we are planting *everything*--carrots, radish parts (tops, middles, and bottoms), onion bulbs, rye grass, and alfalfa. Today we read a story called *What Can You Do With a Yam?* The main idea of the story is that you can grow a plant from a yam. I started my lesson by piquing the students' curiosity shortly after they returned from lunch. On my desk I had placed a large yam, which I promptly and precisely cut in half. As "real" knives are not permitted in the classroom *(I suppose maybe they are for teachers, but I chose to err on the side of caution)*, I used a plastic knife, and said a silent prayer that it wouldn't break. As I rigorously cut my way through the yam, eyes darted around the classroom, watching me with great interest. Then, I placed the yam on a large table beside my desk, a table we often use for science lessons. So what was it? Was it part of my uneaten lunch, or a science experiment waiting to happen? The students weren't sure. When I asked, the opinions were mixed. Suffice it to say, the students were thrilled when they realized it was part of our science lesson. I started by explaining that a yam is a vegetable, and a very delicious one, but it is also something we can learn from in science. I asked the class if anyone had ever eaten a yam. A few students raised their hands, but they were the few who raise their hands for absolutely everything. One sweet young boy raised his hand enthusiastically, but had a tentative look on his face.

> *"I know what they are," he said. "My grandma used to bring them to our house for Thanksgiving, but she doesn't make them anymore, because her husband died...*

So, I said what any quick-thinking first grade teacher would say, "Well then, perhaps your grandmother would like to make yams for our class!" The boy agreed, the class cheered, and I wondered just what I might have gotten myself into with my hasty suggestion. I sent a quick e-mail to the boy's mom:

*"Today we had the sweetest conversation in science. We were talking about yams, and I asked if anyone had ever eaten them. Your son knew about yams right away, and said that Grandma used to make them, but she doesn't anymore because her husband died. He told me grandpa had cancer. It is just heartbreaking to me how many lives cancer touches, even in indirect ways. I'm not sure of Grandma's current health status or where she lives, but if she would like to make yams to serve to our class, we would welcome her visit. Never a dull moment (or a dry eye) in first grade."*

The boy's mom replied, stating that Grandma would *love* to make yams and visit the classroom. She added that her son told Grandma to be sure to use extra brown sugar and marshmallows. As the days passed leading up to Yam Day, my students carefully tended to our growing plants. I notified the office we were going to have a special visitor, and the staff was buzzing with excitement about our unusual snack. I wondered what Grandma must have been thinking as she so lovingly prepared the yams for us. Was it once her husband's favorite dish? Why had she stopped making them? Was she struggling with the sadness that often comes with grief? Was our request for yams a hard one for her? Grandma arrived early on the designated day, casserole dish carefully secured inside a quilted case. She made plenty for everyone and the students were eager to try them. Grandma and I sat at the science table and talked while the children enjoyed the sweet, buttery treat she had provided. I am a picky eater, and have never in my whole life eaten a yam, but this was a special occasion and I needed to try one. They were delicious!

***The wisdom in this story:* "Comfort food is a food item that takes your memory back to a time or place." (Margaret Marshall)**

# *First Day of Fishing*

## Saturday, April 1

I'll always feel a little melancholy on the first day of fishing. Ever since my kids were small, a generous family opened their hearts and their home along the creek to us and invited one and all to come fishing. There were fresh donuts, soggy shoes, and cool crisp mornings. There was laughter, some tears, and a lot of little children learning lessons in patience. It was along the creek that my son caught the big brown trout that was talked about for years, and my daughters touched worms (or didn't). It was along the creek that cousins laughed and played, and children too shy to speak to one another in school teased like siblings. For some, it was all about the fishing, but for most it was about the togetherness. When my husband had to work, I knew that plenty of other dads and grandpas were there to watch after my kids and help them bait their hooks, while I settled in my chair under a warm blanket taking it all in and smiling. As the children grew up, weekends became filled with sports and activities that limited our time together by the creek. Some kids started working jobs, and several went off to college. It became much quieter by the creek. Today, I am still in bed, and the house is quiet — too quiet. My husband and son are working, my oldest daughter is at college, and my youngest is still asleep. I've been complaining about Spring allergies, but I'm pretty certain that was a real tear that just rolled down my cheek.

*The wisdom in this story: I'll always feel a little melancholy on the first day of fishing. I am so very blessed to have such wonderful memories to sustain me.*

# *Love, Hugs, and Cheeseburgers*

## Monday, April 3

After a brief scheduling mix-up, today was the day of my long awaited 6-month mammogram. I had been quite proud of myself, busy with teacher and mom things, emotions intact. I hadn't given much thought to this day, the day I would learn whether or not any evidence of cancer presented, the day that would once again allow me to take a deep breath and relax a bit for another six months. I knew I wanted my husband to come along for the appointment, although I knew there wouldn't be much for him to do but wait. He would be the one to carry the donuts, because above all else at these doctors' offices, I am known as the one who wrote the jelly donut book. I think the title of the book makes people laugh. It makes me laugh, so, of course I bring donuts. Yes, my husband, caregiver extraordinaire who lovingly tended to my every need last year, would come along to carry the donuts. While I know his role is far more significant, I am a strong, independent woman and wouldn't possibly admit that I *needed* him there. I knew it and he knew it, I needed him by my side whatever the news the mammogram may bring. I thought my emotions were intact, but I felt myself unravel a bit when I told my students I would be leaving early for a doctor's appointment. I haven't missed much school this year, so this seemed a little unfamiliar to them. A few looked slightly bewildered, *even though I know some of my silly ones were probably secretly cheering that they could misbehave a little in my absence.* As I observed student reactions, I couldn't help but notice one little boy who appeared close in proximity to my desk. This boy is often in close proximity to me, whether it be at my desk, the carpet area, the reading table, or even on the playground. This boy needs me. This boy is one of those

90

ones who needs a little extra love. In a day when we are more reluctant to embrace children, this boy is one of the ones who need a few more hugs. This boy needs the gentle, calm reassurance I bring to his life, and he reminds me of it often when he looks at me and says affectionately, "Mrs. B loves me." Yes, sweetie, Mrs. B loves you. So, just when I thought my emotions were intact, a six-year-old made me cry. As I walked out of the building on the way to my appointment, I said a quick prayer.

*Dear God. Not this year.*
*I can't "do" cancer this year.*
*There is a little boy who needs me this year.*
*In fact, there are fourteen little boys who need me.*
*Fourteen little boys and six very quiet little girls*
*who make up the most perfect class of twenty.*
*No, God...not this year.*

It was then I realized I was trying to negotiate a plan with God; momentarily forgetting the plan was already made. Somehow, everything is a part of God's plan, as hard as it is for me to sometimes accept. I reminded God that cancer sucks, dried the tears from my eyes, and headed off to my appointment. My husband was there to dutifully carry the donuts. I was registered quickly, and when I took a seat in the waiting room, I realized my husband was not by my side. He was still at the reception desk...talking, laughing. The voices were low and slightly muffled, and I was reminded how a surgeon's waiting room typically has a bit of a silent, somber mood. My husband wasn't just bringing them donuts, he was bringing them sunshine. I heard the word cheeseburger, and when he returned by my side I couldn't help but ask, "why were you talking about cheeseburgers?" It was then that I understood the giggles I heard from the reception desk. Apparently, my husband told the ladies that he hoped the title of my next book would be *Cheeseburgers and Pizza*. While I could eat donuts for breakfast, lunch, and dinner my husband is more of a cheeseburger guy. My once shy husband fits into this place beautifully. These people have become a part of our lives. As I was whisked back to the changing room---another pink gown, and emotions no longer intact---I said a prayer of thanks that I was in a place where I feel so loved. When I walked out of the changing room into a quiet, narrow hallway, my eyes met with yet another familiar face. My radiation tech, someone who had been by my side for thirty-four radiation days, had come upstairs to say hello. She saw the donuts and knew I was in the building. Yes, I am most definitely known as the jelly donut lady! *My husband--he is now cheeseburger guy.* The rest of the day passed by quietly and without incident: a clear mammogram, a good report from the doctor, and a heart full of hope. The doctor was about an hour and a half behind schedule, and apologized profusely when she entered the room. I reminded her she need not apologize, that she was providing comfort to women when they needed it most, just as I had needed her at the time of diagnosis. She said that she had three appointments that took twice as long as she had anticipated. I knew exactly what that meant. Three newly diagnosed patients. *Three.* I felt a lump in my throat, and I found it difficult to make eye contact with my husband. I knew he was thinking the same thing: three women, three families, about to experience what I still describe as my worst awful. However, I was feeling blessed. For me, today was a good day. I am the patient who needs a little extra love, and my day was filled with incredible displays of affection and a whole lot of hugs. I was in a place receiving the gentle, calm reassurance that I needed...and yes, on the way home I picked up cheeseburgers for dinner.

*The wisdom in this story: Just as my students sometimes need a little extra love and a few more hugs, I need the same as a patient. How wonderful that God has blessed us with the ability to love and be loved. That is perhaps the greatest of life's blessings...that, and a clear mammogram result. Life is good.*

# *Autopilot to Radiation*

## Tuesday, April 11

I am certain my car can find this place on autopilot, and as much as I dislike pulling into the parking lot on this warm Spring day, it is much easier to do on a follow-up visit than when I was coming for treatment. For thirty-four days last Spring, I came here for radiation. While I know inside this building hugs and "you look great" comments await me; there is a solemnness I feel, as I know I will share the waiting room with patients in various stages of treatment, from newly diagnosed to dying. How heartbreaking it is to me that anyone must endure the awful that cancer brings to otherwise happy, healthy souls. So here I am, in the third parking space that always seemed unofficially reserved for me, reluctant to go inside. My eyes are one blink away from tears, and my heart is deep in prayer for those in treatment.

*The wisdom in this story: What a difference a year makes. I feel so very blessed.*

# *Bald is Beautiful*

**Tuesday, April 11**

When I was sick, my radiation doctor was very concerned I didn't have a wig. It seems some women are not aware resources are available to cover the cost, and he wanted to be sure I knew he could provide one for me at no cost. He seemed a little surprised when I said I didn't want one, and he gently whispered, "I just want you to feel good about yourself." My mother raised me to believe beauty is on the inside, and while the loss of my hair was devastating, it didn't really hurt my self-image. Today at my follow up, he told me my hair was too beautiful...it looked so beautiful it was perfect like a wig. I smiled to remember the compassionate care I received from him last year. Yes, he is a doctor that cared about everything---my radiation treatments, my skin reaction, my fatigue, and even my hair loss (which really was more about my self-esteem). While my self-esteem never suffered, I was always of the opinion I looked like a sick person...a very sick person. I mostly avoided cameras, as I wanted no lasting images of those days. A breast cancer organization recently released a *Bald is Beautiful* video. I admire the courage of the women in the video, and I am proud to call one of the beautiful bald ladies my friend.

*The wisdom in this story: Yes, bald is beautiful.*

# Care Packages

**Wednesday, April 12**

If there's one thing I always tried to teach my kids when they were little, it was to be appreciative when someone did something kind for them. My daughter's enthusiasm when I send a care package to college far surpasses any small thank you most kids would offer. I think she texts me the minute she returns from the mail pickup location. What a joy to send surprises to my sweet girl!

*The wisdom in this story: "It is not happy people who are thankful, it is thankful people who are happy." (unknown)*

# *Spring Green*

## Saturday, April 15

I had forgotten the beauty of Spring. When I went for an appointment this week, I noticed a beautiful flowering tree in the center of the circular driveway at the cancer center. It was tall and majestic, with delicate white blooms cascading down and blowing in the wind. It was an incredible tree. I can't recall ever having seen that tree in my 34 days of treatment last year. I double checked the calendar, and determined that yes — the tree would have been blooming when I was going for radiation. It seems that those were dark days for me…in so many ways. Yet, just one year later I have again started to notice the beauty around me. White buds stood out to me in particular; as I was reminded of a time I searched endlessly for flowers to decorate the dinner table in an all-white floral theme for my son's senior prom. I blinked away a tear to remember that my son and that sweet girl are no longer together. Yet, somehow — he seems happy, she seems happy. I remember a dear friend once telling me, "You don't get to choose," when it came to our children's decisions of whom to date. Some bright yellow forsythia snapped my attention back into the moment, and I was reminded of forsythia near my old home. How had I not appreciated their beauty when I lived there? Oh, yes — perhaps it was because my husband had to trim them each year. The forsythia seemed more of a curse than a blessing. It has bothered me all week that I didn't notice the tree at the cancer center. How could something so beautiful have eluded me at a time when I most needed to be aware of God's blessings? How thankful I am for yet another opportunity to stop to appreciate the beauty in each day.

*The wisdom in this story: Although I don't always get to choose what happens in life, I recognize that "He has made everything beautiful in its time." Ecclesiastes 3:11*

# *New Homeowner*

**Tuesday, April 18**

I remember the day my nephew was born. I remember seeing him toddle down the aisle at the age of one as the ring bearer in my wedding. I remember belly laughs when he was two and big brother status when he was three. I remember picking 'maters (tomatoes) in Pa Pa's garden with him when he was four. I remember his first day of Kindergarten and the tears I cried when his mother presented him with a box of 64 Crayola crayons just before he boarded the school bus. Twenty years later, I'm proud to say my sister did an incredible job raising this young man. At the age of 25, he is a dedicated employee, a volunteer in the community, and an all around terrific young adult. It was such a joy to photograph my sister standing by his side on settlement day for the purchase of his first home. Most importantly, I'm proud to add that we're practically neighbors, as his home is exactly 3.1 miles (6 minutes) from my house! I pray that his home be filled with lots of laughter, the warmth of family love, the hope of the future, and a garden full of 'maters.

*The wisdom in this story: "Happiness doesn't have just one address." (unknown)*

# *Best Friends Forever*

## Wednesday, April 19

Today I attended the visitation/viewing of someone who was far too young to die. The mother of a former student passed away at the age of 52. Her daughter was in my 1995-1996 first grade class. Her mother was a go-to kind of mom, always wanting to support and show appreciation of teachers. A preschool teacher herself, she loved children, and it showed. As I entered the funeral home, I saw a face that looked familiar to me…another now grown up student. As the two girls embraced and tears started to flow, they both immediately recognized me. I thought 27 years in first grade had aged me a bit, but I looked familiar to them and they were both happy to tell me that they met in Kindergarten and became best friends in my first grade class. Sometimes, the BFF (Best Friend Forever) comments in the classroom while I'm trying to teach reading groups become bothersome. Sometimes the whispers (and even louder giggles) disrupt my teaching. And yet, somehow… friendship and loving one another remains one of the most important things we teach. When I returned back to school, I was a different teacher. I placed this note in the faculty room with a bowl of chocolates:

*Be patient with your students as*
*these early friendships are forming.*
*Someday, these same friends will help*
*one another during life's most difficult times.*

*Please enjoy this sweet treat as I*
*remember the life of someone so dear…*

*Warmly,*
*Michele*

**The wisdom in this story: First Grade Friends are forever.**

# Faster than the Raindrops

**Friday, April 21**

Today I lie in bed, listening to the raindrops, wanting to pull the covers up over my head and rest a little longer. But, today I am driving my youngest daughter to school. It's not because she needs a ride (there's something called a big yellow bus, and also a responsible cousin who drives her regularly). It's not because I'm anxious to try the popular coffee shop's newest drink (it looks disgusting). It's not because it's on my way to work (her school is 20 minutes in the opposite direction). It's not because she asked, but rather because I offered. You see, last year there were days I was too sick to drive her when she needed me. Last year, I watched as my own life passed by in a blur. Last year, I promised myself I would always see the joy in the little things. And last year, I realized the years are fleeting and I need to squeeze as much love as I can into these days. So today, I will drive twenty minutes in the wrong direction to take my daughter to school. I will wait in a very long line for a very overrated "limited time only" coffee shop beverage. I will listen to her stories and smile at her giggles. I will watch her walk into the familiar brick building and know someday I will miss these moments. As I drive myself to school on this rainy day, I will fight hard to keep the tears away, because sometimes my tears flow faster than the raindrops. I cry not because I am sad, but because I feel so very blessed. I need to love my baby girl a little more, before she isn't so little anymore.

*The wisdom in this story: "Let me love you a little more before you're not little anymore." (unknown)*

# Dear Struggling Friend

## Monday, April 24

I have a cancer patient friend who is struggling. She shared her frustration with me, and I tried to find words to comfort her. Inevitably I ended up comforting myself.

*Dear Struggling Friend,*

*Don't be so hard on yourself, and expect that it will be difficult. Your body has been through so much. I worked as often as I felt able during chemo and worked half days during radiation. When I started this new school year, I thought I was "back" in every sense of the word. I wasn't... and it made me angry. My ability to multi-task seemed gone, and simple tasks overwhelmed me. I was at work many nights until 7PM, something I hadn't done regularly since early in my career. I bring more work home now as a veteran teacher than most first-year teachers bring home. All of it exhausts me, and my nighttime sleep is still disrupted, too. But...I kept on going...kept showing up to face each day. I'm not quite sure when things changed for the better, but I'm feeling my confidence return and things get a little easier each day. While I never lost my ability to teach and be competent in my job, it was the small stuff that was hard — the teacher's manuals I read and re-read multiple times, the lesson plans that took too long to write, the papers that were slow to get filed. I learned to make to-do lists to help with forgetfulness, and I learned to adjust my own expectation of what I could accomplish each day. You, dear friend are surely awesome at your job. You will return and you will excel...it just may take awhile. In the meantime, lean on the colleagues who truly want to help lighten your load. It is hard to accept help, but you need to tell yourself it is really okay to admit you need support. You have been through an awful lot. It is okay to feel like you are struggling. Like you, I thought the last treatment and removal of my port would be the closing of a door. It didn't happen. Cancer will sadly always be a part of who we are...we just need to be patient as memory of those hardest days dim. Brighter days are ahead. I love you, friend.*

> *Warmly,*
> *Michele*

**The wisdom in this story: Sometimes I need to heed my own advice.**

# *Happy Birthday to my Gram*

## Tuesday, April 25

Today would have been my grandmother's 102nd birthday. While realistically, she never likely would have lived to be 102, I always wish I could have known her just a little longer. A broken hip from a fall weakened a once incredibly strong lady, and later a blood clot took away the only grandparent I had ever known. When I was a child, my grandmother lived four hours away, but the miles never really seemed to separate us. Sometimes she came to see us, but just as often we went to her house. Her small home was filled with cigarette smoke and her laughter always made me smile. I recall her laughing until she couldn't catch her breath, but all these years later I wonder if was really the cigarette smoke that caused it. I prefer to think it was her laughter. My grandmother's kitchen was small with a table only for two, and I always took my place at the top of the basement steps to eat lunch. I loved sitting on the top step in that little doorway, and when I close my eyes, I can still smell the dampness coming up from the basement below. We ate chip-chopped ham *(I think that's a Pittsburgh thing)*. We also had potato chips with dip and my grandmother always served homemade cookies; I liked her snickerdoodles and raisin best. The town where she lived often felt like a second home to me, even though we really didn't spend any great length of time there. I still feel sentimental and love to reminisce when I go back there. While there were never enough years together, I have fond memories of a loving grandmother. For my own children, my mother's cancer stole the love they were too young to remember.

*The wisdom in this story: Blessed are the grandmothers who spoil and snuggle, hug and hope, boast and brag. And oh, yes...cancer sucks.*

# *The Blue Bins*

**Thursday, April 27**

I still vividly remember the day shortly after diagnosis when I sat at my teacher desk for nearly an hour and wept. I cried because I was leaving students I loved, but I mostly cried because the daunting task of preparing for a substitute (for an absence length yet to be determined) overwhelmed me. I was an expert at writing detailed plans; although I openly admitted that my daily block plans for myself were sometimes sketchy. When you have spent twenty-six years (all but one in the same grade) the details don't seem quite as important to write—they're already in your head. After each and every lesson, a veteran teacher is programmed to reflect and find ways to better meet the needs of her students. Dr. Madeline Hunter's *Essential Elements of Instruction* is still fresh in my mind from my days of student teaching, even though it was so very long ago. I am well aware of the importance of the "seven steps" lesson, and can recite them without prompting: *(Objective, Anticipatory Set, Modeling, Check for Understanding, Guided Practice, Independent Practice, and Closure).* Without a doubt, I believe that I am an effective teacher, and plan appropriately as needed. What I lack in details, I make up for in pretty printer paper, rainbow colored pens, and stickers—always a sticker. However when planning for a substitute, I leave details—lots of details. I write a scripted outline of the day, often telling substitute teachers verbatim what needs to be done. That's okay if you're out for a day, maybe two—but when planning for surgery and a possible sixteen-day absence, well simply the thought of writing such details would make anyone cry. My substitute, with whom I had a friendly yet distant relationship, wanted details. She wanted me to have everything set up and ready for her—*for sixteen days*. My building rep for our local teacher's union told me that the contract required me to write only five days of details before my departure. My husband shook his head and said, "Does she know you are having surgery? Does she know you have *cancer*? Does she realize you're not going to be absent for a trip to Disney World?" Through tears, I answered, "Yes, she knows." To say I wasn't fond of this particular substitute seems unkind, but I tend to be brutally honest when I write. I wasn't fond of her, and her request for more details than my regular block plans seemed rather heartless. I surmised that most sensitive substitute teachers would give me a hug, tell me they would be fine, and then run to the nearest colleague for assistance. I should have written five days of detailed plans and walked out the door. I didn't. I sat at my desk and cried, and then procrastinated until I had no other choice but to write details and organize. When I finished, sixteen bins lined the window counter, one bin for every single day. The bins for the first week were blue—royal blue. They were inexpensive, functional, and filled with everything a substitute would need for each of the days of my absence. As I stared at those bins, tears continued to fall from my eyes. I left school late in the evening, declaring loudly how much I hated those bins. I hated the bins much in the same way I hated hospital gowns, poor hospital décor, and cancer. I said a prayer the substitute would be pleased with everything I had so carefully placed in the bins. For those who don't know the first part of the story, my surgery procedure did not result in clean margins, and on the day I was scheduled to return to work, I returned to the hospital for a second surgery. Again, I filled the blue bins for the substitute. As it appeared my absence would be longer than anticipated, she would need to muddle through the lesson plans while I muddled through chemotherapy. She wasn't pleased my absences would be sporadic rather than permanent. In no time, she found another job, left the district, and a new substitute was hired as her replacement. The new substitute was an immediate breath of fresh air. She cared more about my health and the progress of my treatment than she did about my lesson planning. She told me my block plans were sufficient, and embellished what I provided with her own creative ideas. She accepted my absences were sporadic, instead of permanent, and she stayed by my side through the very end of treatment. She was there when I couldn't be, but understood my need to work, as I felt able. She is now a dear friend. This year, as I struggle to stay organized *(damn chemo-brain)* I pulled out the blue bins. Simply the sight of them gave me a pit in my stomach, as my mind raced immediately to the events of last year. I reflected on the differences between my two substitute teachers. I feel bitter toward the first one, and I doubt she even realizes it. I adore the second one, and pray that I tell her often enough how special she will always be to me.

*The wisdom in this story: The blue bins are now in the big green dumpster at the side of the school. I'm planning to buy some pink bins.*

# *Survivor Year*

**Friday, April 28**

I recently posted this question on social media:

*"Cancer friends---When does the official "survivor year" start? Is it the date of diagnosis, date of last treatment, date of first follow-up appointment, start of post-cancer drugs, or date of first clean scan? My one-year from last treatment is fast approaching and I'm looking for a reason to buy a jelly donut."*

While I received many great responses, these remain some of my favorites:

"Eat the jelly donut just because you can."

"You are a survivor the first breath after you are diagnosed, because you are surviving from that point."

"I think it is really up to you. Groups can set a determining method, but it is what you feel. I started my Survivorship after my last treatment and first clean mark. I don't live in fear, but there is that little voice in my head that reminds me it came back before. I don't really trust it. Get the jelly donut."

"Your reason to buy the donut is because you are a true warrior for the cause."

"One is a survivor at first day of diagnosis! Survivorship is this positive state we just try to honor. Besides, any day is a good day for a donut."

*The wisdom in this story: I like the idea of recognizing a hard fight, but think I like counting the day of last treatment. That was when I felt the cancer was "gone" from my body. I will celebrate my first Survivor Year on May 2.*

# *A Gymnast Story*

## Monday, May 1

When my youngest daughter asked me to find some old photos to help inspire her for an upcoming state gymnastics meet, I had no idea the flood of emotion I was about to experience. I decided to write a story to accompany her photos:

Once upon a time, there was a beautiful little ballerina. She wore ballet shoes, a pink satin costume, and a flower headpiece around her face. When she took her place up on the big stage with all of the other flowers, she was the smallest. Her parents wondered how someone so quiet and tiny could steal the show, but it seemed as if her bright smile told the story. Yes, they just knew they were going to watch this little girl blossom…

After the show ended, the little ballerina decided to try to keep up with her big sister, and bouncing high on the trampoline would be no exception. Thus, a gymnast was born, and once again, her smile told the story.

Soccer, Girl Scouts, 4-H club, and even Dairy Promotion filled her days...but her heart remained in the gym. While some of her friends were cheerleaders and encouraged her to join, she smiled sweetly, and said, "I'm a gymnast."

Eventually, she decided to cheer. Learning to trust others, fly high, and rely on her own strength became important as this gymnast-turned-cheerleader proudly wore her school colors and soared through the years to a coveted Freshman-on-Varsity position.

With the opportunity to cheer on a Varsity team with her sister and an incredibly impressive performance at cheerleading nationals, followed by a little bit of free time on the calendar--her thoughts once again returned to the gym. A list of pros and cons helped her to choose between two things she loved to do...cheerleading and gymnastics... two similar, and yet so very different sports.

My once tiny ballerina grabbed ahold of the ropes in the gym and decided to fly high. From pink tutus and patriotic leotards, to soccer jerseys, Girl Scout uniforms, barn clothes, and a Dairy Miss sash, my little girl embraced childhood wholeheartedly and quietly let others see her sparkle. She proudly wore her school colors of red, black, and white but decided on a different path in a bright blue leotard that made her bright blue eyes appear even brighter. She took the bars, beam, and floor with confidence and as she soared over the vault I realized that my little girl *could* do anything.

Darling daughter, you are a strong woman. You look a challenge in the eye and give it a wink. (Usually with a fluffy white puppy by your side). I admire your strength, courage, and determination. Have a great weekend at States!

*The wisdom in this story: The best is yet to come...*

# *One Year Ago*

**Tuesday, May 2**

One year ago was my last treatment. While I was naïve in thinking the word cancer would never again enter my mind after that day; "Let your faith be bigger than your fear" is what helped me get through my worst awful and is what helps me find the joy in each new day! Thank you to all who continually love and support me. Feeling blessed…

*The wisdom in this story: I am a One Year Survivor!*

# *Teacher Appreciation*

**Monday, May 8**

Happy Teacher Appreciation Week!

Thanks to my **kindergarten teacher** for making everything about school seem magical. Thanks to my **first grade teacher** for teaching me first grade is fabulous.

Thanks to my **beloved middle school teacher** for teaching me to love writing and to have faith in my ability.

Thanks to my **high school yearbook advisor** for teaching me the importance of preserving memories.

Thanks to my **college professors** for teaching me to believe in my dreams.

Thanks to my first **cooperating–teacher** for taking me on as a pre-student teacher and teaching me to laugh when lessons don't always go as planned.

Thanks to **my student teaching co-ops** for walking out the door of their classrooms and giving me the courage to fly on my own.

Thanks to **some amazing teachers** for having faith in me and telling my future principal he should hire me ("just because they said so!")

Thanks to **that same principal** for hiring me, being my first boss, and being the kind of principal who always backed his teachers.

Thanks to my **first-year mentor** for teaching me that just because I love English doesn't mean I should have finished teaching the whole English book by January. Thanks also, for gently reminding me that May might be a little too early to start taking down bulletin boards.

Thanks to a dear co-worker who was once a **first-year-teacher** with me. The late night pizzas and sharing our hopes for the future will never be forgotten, nor will her uncanny ability to imitate every teacher in the building (including me) when our late night sillies kicked in after too many hours at school.

Thanks to **my first students** who have stayed in touch and still tell me they love me all these years later.

Thanks to **a dear elderly teacher** for wanting me to take her first grade position when she retired, and telling the principal he would hire me--or else!

Thanks to **my second principal** for teaching me above all else she wanted me to remember my role as "mommy" to my own children should always come first---even if it might mean she would have to cover my first grade class for a few hours so I could be there for them.

Thanks to **my current principal** for her compassion during my cancer year. Her ability to encourage others to have a growth mindset is inspiring, even on days we feel like we can't possibly grow or give more.

Thanks to **my school secretary, building aides, and school nurse** for helping me pull things together when I feel like everything is falling apart. Thanks for surviving lunch duty and recess duty with me. Thanks for bringing my mail to the classroom and recognizing that to a tired, post-cancer teacher, the office sometimes seems ten million miles away.

Thanks to the **delightful substitute teachers** who took my place when I was too sick to teach, yet graciously stepped aside on days I felt well enough to come to school.

Thanks to **former students** who tell me that because of me, they chose to teach.

Thanks to the **many dedicated teachers** who have taught my own children to love learning.

Thanks to my **sister-in-law** for being "the *other* first grade Mrs. Brymesser" and laughing with me when people get us confused.

Thanks to **my grandmother** who taught in a one-room-schoolhouse, **my cousins**, and my (future teacher) **daughter**, for reminding me that teaching really is in our blood.

Thanks to my **sister and best teacher role model ever** for letting me steal from her files for the past 27 years. Thanks to my sister for also teaching me as a child that even though it's fun to "play school," "playing house" is much, much better.

*The wisdom in this story: I am blessed to know so many teachers and it is a joy to be able to recognize them.*

# *No Place Like Home*

**Monday, May 8**

While I have always loved to travel, I really celebrate a "no place like home" attitude.  When I do travel, I am always eager to pack my bags and even load the car the night before I head home.  I cannot even begin to explain the joy I have felt as week-by-week, carload-by-carload, my daughter has been bringing things home from her first year away at college.  This past weekend, she wanted us to stop by to pick up her dorm fridge.  I told her I probably wouldn't come into the dorm, but rather send her dad in to retrieve the fridge.  She replied, "But you won't ever get to see my dorm room again," which of course made me cry.  So into the dorm I went with my sweet daughter, recalling the carefree days of my own freshman year thirty years ago.  I remembered the empty feeling I had the day I dropped her off last August, and cried a little to know my mother must have once felt the same.  I quietly celebrated that she will soon be home again "for keeps" (or at least until August when she moves into her first off-campus apartment).  I watched her smile warmly at a special roommate, and realized that my daughter knows how to cherish these moments.  Two finals to go and there's nothing left in the dorm room but the sheets on the bed and a laundry bag.  Farewell Harley Hall---there's no place like home!

*The wisdom in this story:  I can't wait to have all my kids back under the same roof!*

# *Long Road Ahead*

**Friday, May 12**

I thought when I had my port removed one year ago it would be like the closing of a door on my cancer year. That didn't happen. While I am now cancer-free, it is hard to admit that I'm still struggling. I recently read an online article, where oncologist Marisa Weiss, MD was quoted:

> *"You're not going to bounce back right away.*
> *You've been hit while you're down so many times:*
> *with surgery and anesthesia, perhaps with multiple*
> *cycles of chemotherapy, perhaps with radiation."*

Yep. Been there, done that.

The article continues to explain the biggest hurdles women face include fatigue, memory deficits, and the inability to focus. Uh-huh.

Weiss observes that breast cancer survivorship is a marathon, not a sprint. It means learning to handle the residual side effects that remain after treatment ends and manage new side effects caused by hormonal therapies, etc.

*The wisdom in this story: The road ahead is a long one.*

# *Happy Mother's Day*

### Sunday, May 14

It is Mother's Day early morning, and my house is quiet—too quiet. Gone are the days of youngsters jumping into bed with me and spilling much of their very best attempt at "breakfast in bed" throughout the bedsheets. Gone are the days of homemade cards filled with crayon scribbles, and promises of feeding the dog and doing other chores without complaint. Gone are the days of "I love you" hand squeezes and bedtime kisses. My kids are all but completely grown—wonderful young adults who make me feel very proud. Yet, sometimes on days like this, I long for the simplicity of childhood. I lie in bed only long enough to realize that no one is in the kitchen preparing a meal for me, and decide that I'll take a long warm shower instead of spending the day in my pajamas. I don't really have a plan for the day. While I love *being* a mom, I miss *having* a mom. As the girls awake, we decide a day trip to Crayola Experience is just what I need today. Research says that coloring can be relaxing, and I don't think you are ever too old to appreciate the scent of new crayons. Our day will be filled with coloring, sculpting, painting, and pretending that we are still five years old. Maybe someone will even make a homemade card filled with crayon scribbles...for me.

***The wisdom in this story: "Artists are just children who refuse to put down their crayons." (unknown)***

# Between the Earth and Sky

## Friday, May 19

There was never a doubt in my mind that my son would grow up to be a farmer. I vividly recall his childhood days, my husband working late in the fields, my son watching from the window and occasionally riding along. We never suggested a chosen career path for our son, things just sort of fell into place that way for him, as he always wanted to farm. We couldn't be more proud. It's a hard life, a humble life, but what better way to spend your days than working God's creation and riding along between the earth and sky on a warm Spring day. I haven't seen my son much lately. Twenty-somethings don't seem to slow down and the farm keeps him busy, too. My husband sent me a picture and a text today, which of course brought a flood of tears to the mama who still finds it hard to believe her babies are all grown up. The picture was of my son on a tractor near a pond by our old farmhouse. The text, "I'm mowing hay down behind our old house, just feeling proud that's our little boy." Yes, our little boy — down behind our old house — working hard in the fields. When I look at the picture, I am reminded of the chubby little blonde boy, now a man, who still finds joy in the simple things.

*The wisdom in this story: Everyone should be blessed to know and love a farmer. I'm the luckiest one. I call him my son.*

# *Just Be There*

## Wednesday, May 24

One of the greatest lessons I learned while sick is that sometimes the best thing one can do for another is to "just be there." While the meal deliveries, cards, and gifts were heartfelt and very much appreciated, it was the people who chose to simply sit by my side and share my sorrow that touched my heart the most. Or the ones who had ever so subtle ways of letting me know they were thinking of me. Last year I wrote about a student who stuck his tongue out at my substitute teacher. This kid was charming. He was missing me, and he was hurting. He was the kind of kid who just needed a little extra love. On occasion, his impulsive behaviors seem to get him into trouble a bit. This morning he appeared in my classroom. I was busy with the hustle and bustle of starting my day and I didn't notice him at first. He stood silently beside my desk, just out of my direct line of vision. When I noticed him, I smiled immediately but felt my eyes fighting the tears. I will always have a special bond with *those* children; the ones who wore pink in my honor and fought the hard fight with me last year. Instinctively, I put my arm around him and gave him a squeeze, even though with today's legalities, it is often best to never touch a child at all. The warmth of my gentle squeeze brought a bright smile to his freckled face, but I could tell he was a bit solemn. He said very little, but politely answered my questions. I thanked him for coming, and told him I love him. I sent his mother an e-mail:

> *"I had the sweetest little visitor this morning…*
> *He didn't say much. I tied his shoe and gave him a hug.*
> *I hope all is well. I sure do miss him."*
> *Warmly,*
> *Mrs. B*

She replied:

> *"Aww, that is wonderful and heartwarming.*
> *He must have just needed a Mrs. B hug, and we sure*
> *miss you. We will always remain in touch as you touched*
> *our lives completely and forever we will cherish the "sick*
> *year" battle won. We will always love our Mrs. Brymesser*
> *and it certainly melts my heart he takes moments to come*
> *hug you."*

I read her e-mail after school and sat for a full five minutes crying, and secretly wondering if perhaps I do need some medication to keep my emotions in check. But, it was then that I realized that I'm not "depressed" or "sad," I am simply deeply touched by the human spirit. I am deeply touched that a simple hug can change someone's day. I am deeply touched that maybe cancer really did teach me something.

**The wisdom in this story:  Just be there — always.**

# *Preschool Graduation*

**Thursday, May 25**

My youngest daughter had the privilege of assisting in a preschool class at her high school this year. While her older sister wants to be a teacher, she has different career aspirations. She told me that she loves children, *which is very evident*, but while she likes playing with them she wouldn't want to teach them — such a wise statement from a young lady. She also told me that she plans to be a veterinary technician instead of a nurse, because she likes animals better than she likes people. I laughed a bit when she said it, but to be honest sometimes I think I like animals better than I like people, too. However, we both love "little people." The joy she has found in the preschool room is immeasurable. Today she was proud to attend the Preschool Graduation. Her enthusiasm for the day was unmatched, as she talked about the event and the adorable girls in their pretty dresses. I don't think she realizes it, but to me her own preschool graduation seems like yesterday. That day, filled with adorable girls, pretty dresses, caps, flowers, first friends, and ice cream cones will forever be etched in my memory.

*The wisdom in this story: "Let them be little. Fill their hearts with laughter. Help them grow wings. Nurture their sense of wonder. Inspire them to believe. Love them like there's no tomorrow." (unknown)*

# *Daisy*

## Thursday, May 25

One of the best things about getting my own first car was choosing a personalized license plate. I chose MLT-86, my initials and high school graduation year. I loved that plate, and all these years later still use it. I've had people ask if I'm a Medical Lab Technician, and some question the significance of the 86. I suppose I never thought back then that upon marriage my initials may change, and I've never changed the plate because it simply reminds me of a younger, more carefree me. My son never wanted a personalized plate, as his practicality won out over vanity. After all, a personalized plate costs extra. Yet, my oldest daughter (who also tends to be practical) was eager to order one. She thought about using her initials, but gently reminded me they may someday change. She thought about using her name, but it was already taken. She chose DAISY, a nickname my mother gave her when she was quite small. DAISY...delicate and simple, yet very strong. Yep, the fitting nickname has served her well through the years, and seemed appropriate for the personalized plate. When my kids were in preschool, they took field trips with their daycare. I never sent them on their way without a guardian angel clip fastened securely to their carseats. Although the silver has since tarnished, the clip has broken, and the wings have become bent...this guardian angel remains in my car. I tried to find one like it when each of my children became licensed drivers, but to no avail. Today, as I watched my husband carefully fasten the new plate to the bumper of my daughter's car, I was reminded of those preschool days. I feel certain Daisy has her very own guardian angel riding alongside of her.

*The wisdom in this story: My mom would have loved this plate. I hope that my daughter keeps it forever.*

# *A Year Full of Memories*

**Tuesday, May 30**

While I am typically more eager than most teachers to take down bulletin boards at the end of the year, removing one titled *A Year Full of Memories* seems a little bittersweet. Last August, I was fighting hard to regain my energy post cancer treatment, and worried what the school year may bring. While I won't say it was an easy year, I feel very blessed to have been able to teach all year (with minimal absences for follow up appointments). It has been a joy to work full time at a school I love, in a classroom that feels like home, with incredible colleagues and students. That said, down with the bulletin board. Only 2.5 days left...and yep, I'm counting!

*The wisdom in this story: "We don't remember days, we remember moments." (Cesare Pavese)*

# *Teacher-in-Training*

## Thursday, June 1

What a joy it was to present my daughter with a keepsake book from my class. I have "Letters from my Students" books from all 27 years of my teaching. My daughter loves reading them and I thought it might be nice for her to have a "Letters for the Teacher-in-Training" book to represent the hard work she did in my classroom this year. She was instrumental in helping me "survive science," served as a Junior Achievement volunteer, and came to talk to students about Summer Safety on this, our last full day of school. My favorite letter to her was scrawled in poor penmanship but deepest meaning:

> *"I think you will be a good teacher because you rock the school. You are going to be the best teacher in the school."*

While it seems my own "best teacher in the school" status is now threatened, I couldn't be more proud. The letters that included "I love you" and "I will miss you" made me cry a little.

*The wisdom in this story: I don't even think my daughter fully realizes the impact she had on my students this year! I am so blessed that she has such a passion for teaching.*

# Counting Sheep

**Friday, June 2**

I stayed up until just after midnight. As I crawled into bed I thought...well, the best part of staying up this late is that I won't be wide-awake at 3AM. Umm. Here it is, 3AM. Wide-awake. Cancer friends, I know you "get it." Oh, how I long for a full night of sleep...

*The wisdom in this story: Sleeping is nice. You forget about everything for a little while.*

# Donuts and Deep Thoughts

## Friday, June 2

Today is National Donut Day, so it seemed only appropriate to bring donuts to school to share with my friends. What a sweet morning to start an otherwise bittersweet day. Today I will say farewell to a special class. I still love teaching. I posted such a comment on a social media page, and a colleague replied with the following:

*"It makes my heart so happy to read this. So many teachers think they can't do it all, but you're living proof that it's possible to be an amazing mama and teacher. To bless and inspire many, many little minds who far too often need us to be their mama, too. I particularly love that you still love teaching despite all the demands we face on a daily basis and aren't afraid to admit it. Thank you for reminding me that even my own love for teaching, that has recently taken a back seat to my new role as a mommy really does still exist. Cheers to another year in the books!"*

It saddens me to know how much teaching has changed since the early days of my career. I completely understand teacher burnout and teachers choosing careers that offer easier work and better pay. While the demands and challenges we face do seem unfair, knowing I made a difference in the life of a child is what matters most at the end of the day.

***The wisdom in this story: Some days I do really struggle to find the delicate balance between work and family — but above all else, family first.***

# *Summer Goals*

**Sunday, June 4**

Summer always feels like a fresh start to me, a time for reflecting, a time for setting goals. This summer, I plan to relax more, worry less, and if all goes well find some front porch time every single day.

*The wisdom in this story: Remember to water the flowers.*

# The Dinner Gong

## Monday, June 5

My mother loved taking something old and making it look new again. It was not uncommon to find her at the table furiously polishing tarnished brass and silver yard sale finds. Somewhere along the way, I inherited her brass dinner gong, which I believe was originally from Germany. Although I loved it as a child, I never quite found a place to display it in my home as an adult. Today, I took the time to finally polish it and display it for use. The rich, hollow sound reminiscent of my childhood makes me smile. While I believe the idea was to ring the gong to signify mealtime, I rang it often...sometimes several times throughout the day, but loudest at dinnertime. With every new effort to focus on relaxing this summer, I hope that the dinner gong at mealtime brings everyone to the table.

*The wisdom in this story: Bless the food before us, the family beside us, and the love between us. Amen.*

# My *"Lived-In" House*

## Wednesday, June 7

My first home was a fixer-upper—a beautiful farmhouse, but a fixer-upper. After seeing it for the first time, I returned to my mother in the comfort of my childhood home and cried. "I can't live there," I said. "It's dirty. It's old. It's in the country." My mother, forever the optimist, loudly proclaimed, "You have love. You will make it beautiful. You will learn to love the country." She quietly added, "It's amazing what a little scrubbing and paint can do." Scrub and paint we did—all throughout my engagement, over a period of weeks if not months, my future husband and I scrubbed and painted. If there's one sure way to find out if you can get along with someone, it's renovating a home. Those days confirmed that we loved one another, and also confirmed we both *hated* painting. A paint bucket falling off of a ladder ledge and splattering to the floor and a paint swatch looking very different from the true paint color were just a couple of our mishaps. But, as with everything else in life, my mother was right, we had love; we made it beautiful. Life in the country became my most perfect place. We filled that house with memories. We brought each of our children home from the hospital to that house and were greeted by a hand-painted stork in the yard reminding us that our lives were becoming even more full. We spent the first fourteen-and-a-half years of our marriage there, and while we could have spent a lifetime in that house, we both had a bit of a yearning for something new. I wanted something clean and fresh, my husband wanting something that needed a little less fix-it-up. We designed the home of our dreams, met with a contractor, and in what seemed like no time we were ready to move into our new home. Our new home was large—extravagant even—but we were a family of five, a family who always welcomed guests. We designed our home with this in mind, a large

128

open floor plan with plenty of room for visitors and no division of our togetherness. When the home was under construction, it became a great place for hide-and-seek. Without furniture and all of our belongings, it looked immense. Oh, how I prayed that inside the walls of the house would someday feel like the home we had dreamed of creating. Shortly after moving day, we hosted an Open House. Our home was buzzing with excitement, and every room was filled with smiling loved ones who had shared life's journey with us. One dear friend I had known since my son was born approached me with tears in her eyes. "You did it!" she said. I thought perhaps she was referring to the construction process being completed, but she continued. "You made this house so cozy—just like your farmhouse. When it was under construction, I was worried you would lose the warmth I felt in your old house. But, you did it! You have created a beautiful, cozy home." I looked around. It *was* cozy. Our home was beautiful, built by a talented custom homebuilder, and could have appeared showcase quality. But I didn't want showcase, I wanted cozy. My friend said we had mastered it! Living in this house for the past nine-and-a-half years has been a blessing. We have hosted countless playdates, birthday parties, sleepovers, hayrides, homecoming dance dinners, cookie baking events, Christmas breakfasts, and prom photos. We have fed the football team, and offered all who visit to pull up a chair and stay awhile. My kitchen chandelier has met with a fast moving soccer ball, and I have indentations in my staircase drywall from a Nerf gun carried by an overzealous middle school student. I'm not happy about it, but I have dog pee on some of my carpets, and dog poop in the dining room. Even on its most cluttered days, I love my home. As my energy levels post-treatment have returned, I find great joy in cleaning and organizing a house I ignored during my illness. I see home improvement projects that need my attention, but I can't help but smile. I feel a little melancholy to know that we will soon tear up the girls Bubble

Gum and Grape Ice colored carpets for a more modern and grownup flooring, but I love our "lived in" house. I will forever be appreciative of our homebuilder's quality craftsmanship and attention to detail. I'm glad we have maintained a wonderful relationship with him through the years. I'm pretty certain we may need him to someday recommend a painter…

*The wisdom in this story: May God richly bless all of your days, and may your faith always be bigger than your fear. May your lives be filled with the laughter of children, the warmth of family love, the fond memories of the past, and the hope of the future.*

# *Blessed Assurance*

## Thursday, June 8

My husband's grandmother lives in an assisted living facility.
She is 95, soon to be 96. My son was born on her 75th birthday,
something she is eager to tell anyone who wishes to hear
about her great-grandchildren. While I know my visits are
never often enough, I try to stop to see her as my schedule
permits. During my cancer year, my mother-in-law was
always eager to tell me grandma remembered to ask about
me, and even when she didn't remember other things, she
always remembered to pray for me. She is a woman of great
faith, and her religion is important to her. I was delighted to
learn the afternoon activity on the day of my visit would be a
hymn sing. The residents gathered in the main lobby, and
songbooks were distributed. Grandma held her book in her
lap, but didn't open it. I never want her to feel incompetent,
so I always ask her if she wants help before I do something for
her. I asked her if she wanted me to help her find the correct
page. She smiled sweetly and said, "no." Her book remained
closed. I knew this woman of faith knew most of the songs by
heart, and I suspected she would sing them loudly—she *didn't*
need a book! They started by asking if anyone wanted to
make a request, and residents called out their favorites…*Sweet
Hour of Prayer, Blessed Assurance, and In the Garden*…three that
just happened to be my favorites, too. What a great day this
would be, feeling grounded by faith, and surrounded by the
elderly. The pianist played loudly, and I could only hear soft
voices in the room. Grandma sat silently. When I touched her
arm she smiled. I sang along, but felt my eyes filling with
tears. Music does that to me. Spending time with old people
does that to me, too. Another lady small in stature but large
in presence, stared at my daughter. This lady was having
trouble turning the pages, and my daughter was happy to
help. At the end of each hymn, the lady passed her songbook

to my daughter silently, expecting the pages to be turned for her. This process continued, and not one word was ever exchanged between the two. They both smiled with their eyes and for a brief moment, their two worlds collided. A beautiful young teen with her whole life ahead of her—and a dear sweet old lady who surely longed for her younger years; a beautiful young teen learning to trust her faith, and a dear sweet old lady relying on her faith. I loved watching this interaction between them. At some point, concerned that Grandma wasn't singing, I realized that the other lady wasn't singing either. In fact, she wasn't even looking at the words in her songbook. She act of passing the book back and forth with my daughter seemed simply a means of shared affection. I started to notice very few of the residents were actually singing. Many simply gazed around the room, and some tapped their hands lightly on the handles of their wheelchairs. Yet, there was such a calming peace in this room. The calming peace that comes with *faith—hope—love*…most definitely love.

> *"Perfect submission, all is at rest.*
> *I in my Savior am happy and blessed.*
> *Watching and waiting, looking above,*
> *Filled with His goodness, lost in His love.*
>
> *This is my story, this is my song,*
> *Praising my Savior all the day long;*
> *This is my story, this is my song,*
> *Praising my Savior all the day long."*
>
> *(Fanny Crosby)*

**The wisdom in this story: On this day, I was blessed with echoes of mercy and whispers of love.**

# *The Vet Clinic*

## Thursday, June 8

I should have known when one of her first words was "moo."

I should have known when she was determined her tiny little legs could keep up with the pace of a pet duck.

I should have known when she was a toddler and rested her head on our puppy at naptime.

I should have known when she found humor in the ornery goats that regularly escaped from their fenced area.

I should have known when she named a cat "Oreo," and allowed it to follow her home in spite of her barking dog and her mother's allergies.

I should have known when she was eight years old, fell in love with alpacas, and declared she "needed" one...or maybe two.

I should have known the first time she embraced a very large animal both willingly and lovingly.

I should have known when she sat in the damp, cold barn with sad eyes (but never a tear) offering comfort to an alpaca in its final days.

I should have known when she stepped into the show ring with a quiet confidence, reminded a young alpaca she was boss, and walked away with a blue ribbon.

I should have known the day she helped her daddy build a fence and then climbed through the fence in her pajamas to feed "her 'pacas."

I should have known when she whispered to a baby bird and held it ever so gently while mama bird watched silently.

I should have known when she put a harness on a young bull, marched him across the street into our yard, and promptly named him *"Hamburger."*

I should have known when she was almost a teenager and wanted a puppy more than an iPad.

I should have known the day she convinced her brother to build a chicken coop out of wood from our old swingset.

I should have known when she convinced her father (who always said, "We will never have chickens.") to get chickens. I should have known when I saw her gently gather eggs and marvel at the wonder of nature.

I should have known when she hand-fed vitamins to a sick chicken daily. That chicken eventually became the longest living chicken in our flock.

I should have known when the farm chore of feeding calves became more of a joy than a chore to her.

I should have known when she told me she wanted to visit a college that offered a veterinary technician degree.

I should have known when I watched her perform pretend EKG's on her puppy, mimicking what she had learned on the college tour.

I should have known when the child who never really liked school signed up for a summer math class to advance her studies.

I should have known, and yet as she spent this evening observing in a veterinary clinic it occurred to me that I didn't see this day coming. I didn't see that the little one who said "moo," walked as fast as the duck could waddle, and rested her head on a puppy at naptime wasn't going to be little for very long. I didn't see that the goats, alpacas, baby birds, chickens, and even the bull needed her more than she needed them. I didn't see that the puppy she so loved as a toddler had grown up right along with her. He is now slightly crippled and partially deaf, and she speaks to him in the same loving, yet authoritative tone she used when she was three. I didn't see that the little girl who never liked dresses really is a "true farm kid" more comfortable in blue jeans and boots (and maybe a pink stethoscope around her neck.) I didn't see that by allowing our girl to spend time with the animals, we were helping to prepare her for a lifelong career. I didn't see that all of it was happening so fast. My baby — the youngest of three — making big, responsible, adult-like decisions. I sat in the parking lot of the clinic fighting to keep the tears away. She came out smiling and talked the whole way home. Favorites included the elderly couple with four dogs, the little boy who cried when told his dog needed a vaccine, and the goats (yes, goats) examined on the back of a pickup truck in the parking lot. Highlights included a dream realized, the opportunity to hold a cat as it was given anesthesia, and the feeling of working in a clinic where rooms were small but hearts were big. I should have known that my sweet, quiet, confident girl would fit right in at the vet clinic. Tomorrow, my daughter will dash across the parking lot blonde ponytail swinging for more observation hours in the clinic. She was invited back — for surgery. The best really is yet to come...

*The wisdom in this story: "Spiritual souls recognize that all animals are spiritual beings." (Anthony Douglas Williams*

# *Bring Your Own Sunshine*

**Sunday, June 11**

One year ago, I had to carefully protect my radiation-sensitive skin from the sun, and didn't really go outdoors much. Today, I sit outside, hair blowing in the breeze loving the feel of the sun's warm rays on my skin. The girls created a synchronized swim routine in the pool, and I'm simply enjoying their laughter. What a difference a year makes.

*The wisdom in this story:  Sometimes you have to bring your own sunshine.*

# *A Letter of Love*

## Wednesday, June 14

A letter arrived in the mail today. I immediately recognized the handwriting, but I also smiled to see the sunny yellow return address label carefully affixed to the top left corner by my dear middle school English teacher. We reconnected last summer and I just love that she wants to stay in touch!

*Monday*

> *Dear Michele,*
> *Just to let you know I'm thinking*
> *of you. I show off your book to everyone —*
> *every chance I get! My friends are* very
> *impressed — — —*
> *I hope you're enjoying your summer —*
> *relaxing and having fun — most of all I hope*
> *you're feeling well —*
>
> *Love,*
> *Mrs. B*

Underneath her formal name, she had written her first name in parentheses. I suppose she was doing it to be casual, but I could never imagine calling any of my teachers by their first name! Yes, no matter how old I am, she will always be my Mrs. B. I looked at the beautiful stationery she used, kid-drawn images of a sunshine (with sunglasses), a rainbow, a cupcake, and a flower. I smiled a little to notice that she had used the notepaper upside down, so the images *(upside down)* appeared at the bottom of the page instead of the top. I suspected she would not be happy to know that she had done this, but simply the fact she is writing to me deserves to be commended.

**The wisdom in this story: Mrs. B loves her students—forever.**

# *Father's Day*

**Sunday, June 18**

Today is Father's Day.  While I sent the obligatory card in the mail to my father, I felt a tear forming in my eye about the somewhat fractured relationship I now have with my father. He doesn't know it.  If anyone asked, my father would likely describe our relationship as "close."  While I think I once felt the same, I can't say the same is true now.  My dad was a provider.  He worked hard every day of his life until his retirement, making sure there was food on the table, a tidy home, gas in the tank of the car he purchased for me, and a paid college tuition bill so that I could simply focus on my studies.  My mother snuck me out on shopping sprees so I had the most perfect wardrobe.  While I used to think he didn't know about our splurges, I suspect he had some idea where the money was coming from when his teenage daughter was always impeccably dressed.  My father hosted my beautiful wedding reception and shook his head when I tried to be practical.  Nothing was too costly for his daughter.  We danced to *Daddy's Little Girl* and we both had tears.  I was privileged— spoiled even, never wanting for a thing.  My dad became beloved Pa Pa to each of my children, and doted on them in a way such as one might expect from a proud grandparent.  After my mother's diagnosis (Stage 4 colon cancer) he helped pay daycare costs for my children, as it was heartbreaking to him that Grandma and Pa Pa could no longer babysit.  My father was a wonderful caregiver to my mother during her illness, tending to every wound and physical need. I can't help but think she was a little lonely during that time, as his interactions with her were mostly of the caregiver type, methodical and scheduled.  He kept detailed notes about her medications, food intake, and physical discomfort to share with the Hospice nurses.  While he sometimes seemed a little distant, I suppose that may have made things easier for him knowing that there would be no recovery, but rather a slow decline for my mom. My father's life must have been a little too empty for his liking after her passing. He remarried, put the house on the market, and moved back to his hometown. My father did little to include my sister and me in his relationship with his new wife, and we were not invited to their wedding. It was a small ceremony with only his wife's sister, but to feel excluded was hurtful. He found it difficult to understand why we weren't always eager to go to dinner when he was in town, and awkward conversations sometimes turned into arguments. I am stubborn and opinionated, and I suppose he is, too. I feel certain that I remind him a lot of my mom, in both appearance and attitude. I don't think he could handle that I was no longer the little girl who simply said "yes, sir" and dried my tears upon command. I had opinions, feelings, and I often said exactly what was on my mind. My father was not quite willing to admit how much our lives had changed with my mom's passing. To say that she was the glue that held the family together would be an understatement. My own family and I went from seeing my father on a daily basis to seeing him once, sometimes twice a year. Our relationship is not "close," and it's not only due to proximity. I know it and he knows it. Yet, he is my father, and I was taught respect. So the card and the check are in the mail as we celebrate Father's Day. Then I look at the man I married. I married the most wonderful man. This man has been by my side through car seats, strollers, and sixteen-year-old drivers. This man has helped feed babies, feed the football team, and (in his role as dairy farmer) feed our community. This man opens his heart and his home to everyone, and simply smiles when my kids bring friends through the door. This man has been by my side through all of the tears and joys of parenting, and holds my hand when through each milestone I realize our kids are growing up too fast. This man has taught my kids strength, determination, a good work ethic, and unconditional love. This man knew how to be a caregiver to me during my illness without making it seem methodical and scheduled. Through all of life's adventures, this man is the one who reminds me to slow down and see the rainbows.

*The wisdom in this story: The only thing better having my husband as my spouse, is my children having him as their Daddy.*

# *Southern Accent*

## Sunday, June 18

We just enjoyed a long weekend away. We left Thursday, traveled to Virginia, and spent the night in a hotel. We arose early the next morning and drove to North Carolina, where we stayed until mid-day Saturday. We traveled back through Virginia, spent the night and returned home Sunday evening. We were gone from our home four short days. Upon arrival home, my youngest daughter announced: "I do believe I picked up a bit of a southern accent."

*The wisdom in this story: Never doubt how entertaining life is with my youngest child.*

# The Pediatrician's Office

**Monday, June 19**

I'm at the Pediatrician's office for my daughter's annual wellness checkup, watching what seems like a never-ending stream of babies and toddlers enter the waiting room. The growing up years of my own children almost feel like a bit of a blur, and I look longingly at the baby carriers and diaper bags. I realize that in two short years, my daughter will age-out at the Pediatricians office and be considered an adult. I wonder how the years have passed so quickly.

*The wisdom in this story: I need grandchildren!*

# *Turning Twenty-One*

**Tuesday, June 20**

I turned 21 on a Monday night. I was in college—a sorority girl—and *everyone* went *out* for their twenty-first birthday, *even if it was on a Monday night.* We went to a local bar in town first. It was a beer-only type of place but the owner was always there to serve a cold one, and he celebrated 21st birthdays with bottle opener key chains and mugs for the really special customers. Apparently, I was a really special customer; I got a keychain *and* a mug. While I spent a lot of time there for the remainder of my college years, I don't think I was quite mug-worthy. I was tiny and cautious, and sipped more than I drank. But, back to the birthday: After the bar we went to a second place known for their appetizers and great food, but also plentiful in beverage choices. It was there we encountered another lone birthday celebrant with his group of friends, and I think they thought we needed to match one another in shots. They bought me fruity flavored drinks with cute names, and laughed when someone suggested another round. It was a night of bad decisions, but my friends insisted you only turn 21 once. Thankfully, I didn't get sick, and aside from drinking a bit too much, didn't do anything I would have later regretted. Fast forward to present. My son is turning 21…on a Tuesday. My husband has the fridge stocked with beer and a bottle of my favorite peach schnapps. We struggle to stay awake until my son comes home from work and greet him with his "first" beverage just after midnight. Later today he had a lunchtime beer with his cousin, and two enthusiastic ladies at the restaurant bought him a shot, undoubtedly reminiscing about their own turning-21 experiences. We visited a beer distributor, where I became fast friends with a guy who looked like he drank as much beer as he sold. We shared stories, and he gave my son a keychain.

Apparently, my son was a really special customer. He got a keychain, a t-shirt, two cup koozies and a cooler bag. Yep. This guy could probably tell my kid drinks more than he sips. I took my son to the liquor store, where he never even got carded. After I insisted that the store clerk ask for ID, he was wished happy birthday one last time before heading home, but not without a "please be safe" speech from the store clerk who is also a father. While today probably wasn't my son's ideal way of celebrating turning 21, I felt glad to be included. It was a special day, one we will both always remember. I do believe the highlight of his day may have been the keychain. Then again, the ladies who bought him a shot (*a very expensive shot*) were pretty memorable, too. When I look at this handsome young man drinking a beer in my kitchen, it's hard to believe it's the same little boy who once fetched a beer from the fridge for his dad on lawn mowing days. I know there will be beer-only bars in his future. I know he will visit places with appetizers, great food, and plentiful beverage choices. I know his friends will buy him shots and he will laugh when someone suggests another round. I know he will have a night of bad decisions, but his friends will insist you only turn 21 once. I pray he doesn't get sick, or aside from drinking a bit too much, do anything he will later regret. Celebrating his 21st, and remembering my own, makes me wonder when birthdays stopped becoming important to me. There were years when I would even cringe a little when someone told me Happy Birthday. I didn't like being the center of attention. Yet, now — the post-cancer me — wants to tell the world when it's my birthday. I feel certain I deserve to be celebrated. I will turn 50 on my next birthday. Perhaps my celebration will need to include fruity flavored drinks with cute names and laughter with each new round. My good friend at the beer distributor may even give me a key chain.

**The wisdom in this story: Drinks on me.**

# *Rosenthal China*

## Thursday, June 22

Over ten years ago, with tears streaming down my cheeks, I packed up my mother's fine china as my father sold my childhood home and moved away. For over ten years, that china has remained in the same bubble wrap and tissue paper in which it was placed on one of the saddest days of my life. A few years ago, I was feeling sentimental at Christmas time and sent my son to the dining room to find and retrieve the gravy boat and mashed potato bowl from the endless stacks of bubble wrapped china. He was gone awhile, and returned to tell me he thought it was safest to keep that china packed away. This summer, I decided to unwrap it all, wash it to its original splendor, and properly store it in quilted pouches. My oldest daughter loved the china and was delighted to know my mother had purchased it in Germany. She told me we should use it everyday. After a bit of contemplation we agreed that nothing should be too pretty to use only on holidays. We decided the 22nd of every month would become our "china day" and no matter the meal, we would use the beautiful white dishes. I quickly envisioned peanut butter and jelly sandwiches in the dining room and smiled to know my mother would approve, but only if I used Jif. Tonight is the first of what I hope truly does become a tradition. On the menu: chicken and shrimp pasta alfredo, steamed broccoli, and garlic bread. Feeling blessed.

*The wisdom in this story: Use the china — always, or at the very least once a month.*

# *We Still Do*

**Monday, June 26**

Twenty-four years.

To have and to hold from this day forward:
For better — *the birth of my babies*
For worse — *the death of my mom*
For richer — *still waiting for that to happen*
For poorer — *daycare, braces, mortgage, cars, college*
In sickness — *cancer sucks*
In health — *nothing better than healthy kids*
For as long as we both shall live.

Twenty-four years.

Two homes. Eight cars. Three kids. Three dogs. Two goats.
Three ducks.  Two alpacas. Five chickens. Too many goldfish.
Home cooked meals. Dinners out. Staycations. Vacations.
Many tears but more smiles. Many heartaches but more joys.
Acting tough but being tender. I need him, he needs me.

Life is good.
Twenty-four years since we said "I do."

**The wisdom in this story:  We still do.**

# *First to Punch*

**Tuesday, June 27**

I received many heartfelt, thoughtful greeting cards when I was diagnosed with cancer, and reading them brought me great comfort. While I loved all of the cards, one was by far my favorite. The sentiment:

> *Please let me be the first to punch the next person*
> *who tells you everything happens for a reason.*
> *I am sorry you are going through this.*
> EMILY MCDOWELL

This card was sent to me by a retired teacher friend who has an incredible gift for showing kindness, reading books to children, and selecting perfect greeting cards. So the *"let me punch"* card coming from her surprised me a bit, but she had her own experiences with cancer, and certainly a fighting attitude. My friend lives in Maine now and I miss her. I loved the card so much I had it enlarged to 16x20 for an end-of-treatment donut party in my home. Now, one year later and on a quest to clean and organize my life, I couldn't bring myself to toss it. I ordered a beautiful, distressed frame, and have the perfect spot to hang it just outside my master bedroom closet door. I will see it every day, pause, laugh a bit, and remember how blessed I have been to be so deeply touched by the kindness of others.

*The wisdom in this story: If someone in your life is struggling, please reach out to him or her. It's okay to simply give a hug and even say, "I have no words." Please do your best to refrain from saying "everything happens for a reason." My friend and I just might be around the corner listening and ready to punch!*

# *Oncologist*

**Thursday, June 29**

Oncologist. Routine follow-up. Love the people, hate being here. While I understand the need for follow-up appointments, simply walking through the doors of a place I visited during my most awful days isn't easy. Today, a different face greeted me at the reception desk. She was pleasant enough, but not familiar. Oh, how slow I am to embrace change. Check-in was without incident, and with every quick update of insurance I count my blessings that I have excellent medical coverage. I found a seat in the waiting room and smiled to recognize that most of the people here today looked healthy — at least none of the telltale signs of side effects of chemotherapy. They called my name quickly for bloodwork, and I silently praised myself for drinking a full bottle of water before arriving. I was once told that being fully hydrated helps make a blood draw easier in a patient with small, difficult veins. Yet, as always — I am the tricky patient, and not one but two individuals had to try to draw blood from my arm, while I tried to look away and ignore the fact that I was likely going to develop a slight bruise after leaving. Just as I closed my eyes I heard a familiar voice…a nurse…my nurse…my chemo nurse…my chemo angel. It takes such a special person to be a nurse, and my chemo nurse is the absolute best. During my treatment days, she was caring and concerned without being overbearing. She came and went from the room almost methodically without making it feel intrusive. Today she came to say hello, and I had a difficult time finding my words. We hugged, of course — because these people become like family to you during treatment. I whispered to her how much I still feel like I'm struggling emotionally. I knew she would "get it." Mid-whisper, I looked up to see my oncologist nearby. While I know she wasn't eavesdropping, I feel certain the look in my eyes and my nurse's expression indicated that residual cancer crap is still with me…some physical, some emotional and most all of it difficult to explain. I retreated to the waiting room, which was almost empty by then, something for which I felt grateful. The waiting room was always the hardest place for me when I was sick…a place with patients in various stages from newly diagnosed to dying. In the exam room, my blood pressure was elevated but only slightly, and I was reminded of how much I hate anything medical—even follow-up appointments. It's funny, but I really can't remember much of what I talked about with the doctor. Last Fall she had recommended a counselor who specializes in cancer survivors, *if I felt the need to see someone.* I'm certainly not "anti-therapy" but to be honest a morning of prayer, a hug from family, lunch with a good friend, and writing stories seems to help me cope. She mentioned again that counseling was available. Yep, she most definitely overheard my conversation with my nurse. Nope, I'm not in denial. I really don't think I need counseling. I pretty much told her the same. I have faith, family, friends, and page after page of story. She smiled gently, and I was again reminded of why I love her. I told her I didn't want to have to start over and tell my story to a counselor. Sometimes not thinking about cancer is easiest. She said the story isn't the important part, but rather how we deal with what we have been through. Hmm, I'm not sure I liked that answer. I think my story *is* important, and well, donuts are pretty much how I deal with what I have been through. I thought about her words on my ride home. Really, donuts help—but how *have* I been dealing with the after treatment part of cancer? Well, I think I'm living each day like it could be my last, and counting every single blessing. I think I'm laughing more, and worrying less. I think I'm appreciating knowing that on the other side of my darkest days, I have found sunshine.

**The wisdom in this story: Faith, family, friends—and donuts.**

# *Parenting Fail*

### Thursday, June 29

Sometimes as parents, our absolute ugliest comes out. Today was a hard day for me, and most definitely not a parenting win. The subject was laundry, and the grand finale of the evening was a family meeting with two somber looking young adults seated on the fireplace hearth and a tired teenager falling asleep in the chair while mom rambled on…and on…and on…for what seemed like forever. In my house, the kids all started doing their laundry sometime around the middle school years. For each, the routine is a little bit different. The oldest has double the task, washing his regular clothing and then also his barn clothes. The middle child methodically sorts and separates her darks, lights, and delicates. Her process is efficient, and after each load is completed, she folds it all and puts it away. The youngest waits until there is literally nothing left in her closet to wear and washes large loads, which get tossed back into the hamper and worn later in a somewhat rumpled fashion. My husband washes his own barn clothes, and does his best to help me with our laundry basket and never ending flow of towels and washcloths. My own laundry style is disjointed. While I strive to have the same efficient process my middle child follows, it seems I'm never home long enough for a load to get through the wash-dry-fold process. Therein lies the problem. My son has a habit of tossing his finished laundry (regular or barn clothes) into a laundry room cubby. He also tosses anything that has not been removed from the dryer into a cubby. Now, for those who have never washed barn clothes, I believe there is a proper way of doing that, too. Early in my marriage, I worked carefully to keep my husband's barn clothes clean and fresh. I started with a half-filled washing machine set on the hottest cycle and more bleach than one should probably ever use. I called that the pre-wash. Next, I ran those same clothes through regular cycle with bleach, detergent, and fabric softener. While my husband's barn clothes smelled good, after some time they became full of holes. He wore them anyway. Years later, life caught up with me, and my husband and son began washing their own barn clothes. Our new front-load washing machine made it more challenging to pre-wash in my usual way. The manufacturer boasted that one could efficiently wash sixteen pairs of jeans at once. They forgot to specify in the manual that sixteen pairs of *barn* jeans may not be a good idea, but that's what my guys do. They pack the washing machine as full as possible, sometimes so tightly I'm surprised the clothing even gets wet. It has a distinct smell when finished...a barn smell mixed with the slightest aroma of detergent. However, it seems silly of me to complain, as I know some men have never in their lives done a load of laundry. So, today had been a difficult day. The oncology follow-up brought back a flood of emotion, and I was feeling a little delicate. I was just kind of going through the motions of after-dinner cleanup, my mind somewhere else. When my youngest child dried her hands on her sister's shirt, I was reminded my kitchen towels had never been retrieved from the dryer. As I entered the laundry room, I found a large basket with clean clothes tossed on top of dirty, and two of our three cubbies overflowing with a mix of laundry that belonged to everyone. Well, everyone except the middle child, who had folded her laundry and put it away. I looked at the piles and started to cry. Then I became angry. I started to yell — at all three kids. Words came out that I never intended to speak — ugly words. I had spent all of my years as a mother ensuring my children were well cared for and clean. *They might have grown up on a farm, but they didn't grow up smelling like a barn.* It was inconsiderate, disrespectful, for them to have tossed my efforts at laundry aside. How dare they be so careless? How dare they create more work for me? Would their friends like it if they smelled like the barn? I think not. I expressed my dissatisfaction — repeatedly. As my bewildered looking children sat and respectfully listened to me rant and ramble, it finally occurred to me that this wasn't about the laundry. As always, I was mad at the cancer. It seemed easier to be mad about the laundry (something we could control) than to fret and cry about the way cancer (something we couldn't control) had invaded our otherwise happy lives. My kids looked solemn and sad, but at times looked like they were trying not to laugh at me. I was truly acting like a nutcase. I knew it, and they knew it. When it was evident my messages had been heard and we were all exhausted, I dutifully dismissed my children and they quickly retreated to their bedrooms. I sat silently on the couch, my face buried in my favorite blouse and tears falling onto an unfolded pile of towels. My blouse smelled like the barn. Damn cancer.

*The wisdom in this story: Tomorrow will be a better day.*

# *Gettysburg*

**Friday, June 30**

In the 21 years I've been a mother, I have never (ever) had the desire to tour Gettysburg Battlefields, and yet I can't think of anywhere I'd rather be on this 90+ degree day than doing the auto tour with my college girl who loves history. *Well, maybe shopping at the Gettysburg Outlets with little sister in the backseat who likes shopping more than storytelling sounds a little more desirable,* but I do have a new respect for the battles fought here and the beautiful countryside just down the road from where I work and live.

*The wisdom in this story: "My brave boys were full of hope and confident of victory..." (George Pickett)*

# *Empty Nest*

**Friday, June 30**

Finally the first moment of Summer I've had time to sit down and enjoy a book…and I'm crying. Recommended by a friend, the book is a collection of a mother's reflections. I've only read the foreword, and I can already tell it's a must-read for all of us with grown children. My nest is feeling empty this evening. I reflect briefly on my own writing and treasure the memories of days gone by...

*The wisdom in this story: Everyone should publish a book— or at the very least keep a journal.*

# Sunrise and Iced Tea

## Saturday, July 1

Someone special came into my life shortly before I was diagnosed with cancer. I visited her when she was admitted to the hospital after my diagnosis. I was there to visit her, but she made it clear that she was going to care for me. I will never forget feeling terrified about what may lie ahead for me, and she said, "Ask me anything, darling." Just her presence in my life helped me feel calm. All during my treatment, this lady texted me "Good Morning, Sunshine" messages. Although her treatment remains ongoing, she posts regular updates on social media. Here is her post from today:

*"It's Saturday, and I am enjoying the sunrise and a glass of iced tea. So glad to have my hubby at home. I feel very blessed with my family. They help me everyday to keep up with this world. God has placed everyone in our lives for a reason. We must love others as we love ourselves. Give often, love more, be happy with ourselves, and always know God is with us. May you have a safe and happy weekend."*

What a joy it is to know her and what wonderful words of wisdom she has to share.

**The wisdom in this story: Some days I don't want to get out of bed. I think I need to try a glass of iced tea at sunrise.**

# *Whatever Your Circumstances*

**Sunday, July 2**

Today at church we studied Genesis 22:1-14, and the sermon was titled *Abraham's Exemplary Faith.* I listened intently, and took notes in the sermon notes bulletin provided by our pastor. A summary of the notes and my reflection follow:

Faith is *believing* God's promises and *acting* accordingly.

Abraham knows two things:
1. God has been *faithful* to him in the past.
2. He is faced with an *unforeseen* and *unfair* tragedy in the present.

As I listened to the story of Abraham's unwavering faith, I began to cry. Sometimes my emotions and tears in public embarrass me, but at this moment, I felt the pastor was speaking directly to me. He said, "This is not just Abraham's story, it is our story. Whatever your circumstances or mine may be, God will provide. No matter what, you will be able to count on many, many blessings from God."

Faith is a journey that involves *hesitation* and *questioning.* It doesn't come easily.

Faith trusts God to do what God promises to do, even when it seems *impossible* from a human perspective.

When diagnosed, I failed to recognize God has been faithful to me in the past. I was faced with an unforeseen and unfair circumstance and I was distraught. My journey involved hesitation and questioning. Recovery and healing once seemed impossible, but with faith, I am trusting God.

*The wisdom in this story: "May we walk by faith, trusting everything that God provides." (Pastor Denny Keller)*

# *Favorite Holiday*

## Tuesday, July 4

A month or so ago, my youngest daughter informed me that the 4th of July is her favorite holiday. She is a shopper, and the stores are filled with patriotic décor this time of year. She told me she just *loves* the colors red, white, and blue. *I just love her enthusiasm.* She told me we should have a party. I responded that several years ago we celebrated the holiday by inviting another family over for a cookout. I suggested that I could call them again. Hmm, she pondered a bit before replying that we should have a party with my sister's family. I agreed, and told her I would invite them. She hesitated. "Well, I think we should have a party at *her* house." I laughed out loud and tried to delicately explain that you simply don't invite yourself to have a party at someone else's house. But this wasn't just any someone else, this was my sister — and she is one in a million. I made the phone call; we invited ourselves, and planned a cookout. It was an incredible day. As I sat on my sister's lovely patio watching her kids and mine float in the pool, I was reminded of days gone by when they weren't so grown up, and gatherings weren't so quiet. I remember the joy on my mother's face when they all arrived at her patio party wearing red, white, and blue. For a few years after my mother's passing my sister and I continued to get together on the 4th of July, Labor Day, and Memorial Day, but then at some point our picnics stopped. I feel so blessed that my daughter's favorite holiday is the 4th of July. I feel so blessed to know that she loves the colors red, white, and blue. I feel so blessed she suggested we have a party. My sister is the best hostess…

*The wisdom in this story: Sometimes traditions lost need to be revisited — even if you decide to invite yourself!*

# No Rest for the Farmers

**Tuesday, July 4**

Some people may resent working while the rest of us celebrate our nation's independence, but not our farmers. While we enjoy hot dogs and hamburgers, they are busy in the fields. God bless my son who thought to adorn the tractors with flags in honor of this special holiday. He is most definitely a proud American and I'm a pretty proud farm wife and mama.

*The wisdom in this story:  Thank a farmer.*

# *A Huge B\*\*\*\**

**Wednesday, July 12**

Social media has become an incredible outlet for those who like to write personal blogs, and it goes without saying, breast cancer patients like me to write stories. We write in fear, we write in sadness, sometimes we even write to ask forgiveness. In one of my favorite articles, *"8 Things People with Cancer Really Want to Say,"* Mailet Lopez reminds us being honest about our feelings is important. Based on input from the cancer community, a list of eight things most want to say was compiled. While I could relate with all of the items on the list, number eight simply resonated with me the most.

*#8. "Life with cancer is an emotional rollercoaster. The kind that goes upside down and leaves you hanging with the blood rushing to your face for awhile – so yeah, I might be optimistic one day and a huge b\*\*\*\* the next. It happens."*

**The wisdom in this story: To those friends who chose to stay by my side (#4) while I was optimistic one minute and a huge b\*\*\*\* the next (#8), my new normal is very scary (#1) and I wanted to let you know I feel blessed to have you as a friend.**

# *Compassionate Care*

## Wednesday, July 12

Last Summer, I was mentally and physically exhausted from a year of treatment. I was very emotional, fragile even. I was trying to feel normal, yet a paralyzing fear of recurrence was always with me. Wanting to ignore my routine health visits, but knowing the importance of keeping up with my gynecological care, I scheduled my annual appointment. I wasn't going to see just any doctor; I needed to select a special one. My year had been difficult, and I needed the best. I needed compassionate care. My thoughts turned quickly to the doctor who had delivered my youngest child. I vividly recalled him sitting in the chair of the hospital room holding my newborn. He stayed — a long time. At a certain point, my husband and I began to wonder if other women in labor might need him, so we asked. He told us his shift had already ended and he loved holding babies. We were simply in awe. This was the doctor I needed to show me care and compassion after my cancer year. On the day of my appointment, I made sure I had current photos of my children in my wallet. This doctor needed to know that the child he had delivered fifteen years earlier was an incredibly sunny spot in my life during my cancer year. However, there was no time for chatting. My doctor seemed disinterested in me as a patient with feelings. He sort of summed me up as someone at great risk for uterine cancer due to my obesity *(damn donuts)* and use of an estrogen blocker drug *(prescribed by my oncologist and used to prevent cancer cells from growing)*. My experience in the doctor's office was awful. After a cancer treatment year of wonderful providers and warm and loving care, my gynecologist seemed unkind, harsh even. It wasn't exactly what he said, but how he said it. My letter of dissatisfaction to the office met with a reply letter that seemed almost patronizing. Tears in my eyes

I vowed I'd never go back. I talked to everyone I knew about my disappointment. I wrote an unforgiving story about the doctor. I cried a little, and then cried a lot. My friends talked favorably of a different doctor in the same practice. They urged me to see her. My oncologist and breast surgeon said the same. 23+ years of good care made it seem reasonable to consider staying. This doctor loved by so many was my age. We had gone to the same middle school and high school. I knew her then, but not well. I saw her once when I was in labor with my youngest child. She entered the delivery room looking sleepy, wearing a rumpled college sweatshirt, and chewing bubble gum. I felt pretty certain she was still the young girl I once knew and most definitely not qualified to be my doctor. I never could have been more wrong. Today was my appointment, and she represented everything I love about quality patient care. She listened intently, smiled appropriately, and offered words of reassurance when I expressed concern. According to those in the medical field, she knows her stuff. It seemed as if when I wasn't looking she had moved on from middle school and high school. She had traded her rumpled college sweatshirt for professional dress and cute shoes. She had aged ever so slightly and beautifully. Her eyes sparkled with compassion, and she asked me about my family — my kids. I felt tears forming in my eyes a bit when she mentioned a classmate recently diagnosed with breast cancer. I didn't ask for details, as I didn't want to put her in an uncomfortable position with doctor-patient confidentiality. Yet, at that moment she wasn't speaking to me as a doctor but rather a person she once knew in school. Even though those school days were a long time ago, I like to think we're both still quite young. I look forward to a long-term doctor-patient relationship with her in the years to come. I might even buy her a birthday gift. I'm thinking a pack of grape bubble gum might be appropriate.

**The wisdom in this story: We're all just kids who grew up way too fast.**

# *A House Full of Windows*

### Thursday, July 13

At the start of Summer, I vowed I would sit on at least one of my three porches every day this summer. That worked out quite well until the temperatures reached the 90's. Suffice it to say, I really like air conditioning. Today I am inside, but I cannot help but look out to appreciate my beautiful view. I am in my favorite room in the house — the sunroom. Three sets of French doors and a patio sliding door grace this room and the sunshine pours inside. My house is quiet at the moment, and I relish in my thoughts. The slightest breeze outside makes the purple coneflowers and white hydrangea gently blow. My grass is a bright green, flanked by an alfalfa field and even further in the distance a fast-growing cornfield. There is a tall, majestic oak tree along a dirt tractor path that I admired years before my home was even built on this lot. The trees on the mountain in the distance are full and lush. The clouds in the sky appear painted. Shortly after my mother passed away, I used to tell my kids, "Grandma in Heaven painted the sky for us." Today, I think she painted everything I am seeing. I am truly sitting here in a location she once called a little piece of Heaven. I love my house, I love my life.

*The wisdom in this story: "May your walls know joy. May every room hold laughter and every window open to great possibility." (unknown)*

# Small Choices, Saved Lives

**Thursday, July 13**

How many times in life do we think of the what-if scenarios? Usually, it's when something tragic could have happened but didn't that we remember to count our blessings. I think of the events of 9/11 and the individuals who weren't in the presence of the attacks because of a small choice they made that ultimately saved their life. A national news media called this *Small Choices, Saved Lives* and reported a story about an executive who rarely left her office but took a walk on 9/11 because it was a calm day with clear blue skies. The report tells of others who took a different subway route or woke up late because of the previous night's football game on TV — choices that made the difference between living and dying. There are stories about cancelled travel plans, phone calls that delayed departure, and people who were simply blessed to miss the tragic events by a mere five minutes. One survivor tells of others swarming her with tears and hugs. "God has a plan for you," they told her over and over. "You were meant to be here." Sometimes I reflect on the what-if scenarios when I realize if things had happened only slightly differently, my life would have been affected by tragedy. Today was one of those days. Today, I was immediately reminded to stop and count my blessings.

*The wisdom in this story: "Every day people make thousands of small forgettable decisions. But sometimes those seemingly inconsequential decisions make the difference between living and dying. A brush with tragedy can leave you fundamentally changed." (Madison Park)*

# *Stole my Happy*

**Saturday, July 15**

*My husband is mowing the grass,*
*my son is pressure-washing the house,*
*my daughter and I are cleaning,*
*and my youngest daughter just brought*
*a little of the beautiful outdoors inside.*
*I love a Saturday at home!*

Moments after I wrote the above on social media with a photo of a beautiful flower arrangement made by my daughter, my son came inside to tell me a friend was on the porch. The friend was a football mom, someone I had grown to love when our boys played football together. Our paths hadn't crossed much lately, although her son was at my house just two weeks ago and I sent her a friendly text. I suggested we get together soon. She was on a bike ride on this beautiful day, and at first our conversation was lighthearted and simple. Then she asked how I have been doing. It felt good to smile and say, "I'm doing really well. I've had two clean scans and my energy levels have returned. I'm doing great." *(Sometimes I feel like if I say it often enough even I will believe it.)* Her smile softened, her expression changed. I saw a familiar look of fear in her eyes. The words that followed were heartbreaking. She told me she had just been diagnosed with breast cancer, surgery planned for later this month. Damn cancer. My friend — another family — devastation — hard times ahead. Cancer sucks. I still smell the aroma of freshly cut grass and the wet siding appears to glisten in the sunshine. Indoors, I know that my home smells of lemon cleaner and freshly cut flowers. It is Saturday and I am at home, but cancer stole my happy. I fight to keep the tears away, but after my friend leaves I fall apart. Please, God — not another.

**The wisdom in this story: In a moment, cancer changes lives.**

# $2^{nd}$ *Street*

## Sunday, July 16 (3AM to be exact)

When you're cruising $2^{nd}$ Street in the city at 2AM because you hate to see your son and a friend pay $30 for transportation: You're proud they make responsible choices and choose designated drivers instead of dangerous paths, but you can't help but feel you're probably the only middle aged parents cruising the block and still carpooling adult "kids." The traffic light changes and you see it—a familiar car—a familiar mom—a mom you spent countless hours with in the high school parking lot waiting for kids to emerge from football and cheer practice. You laugh out loud. You feel more than a little stressed in the $2^{nd}$ street traffic and decide that perhaps next time you will have to meet for coffee to pass the time while the kids are at the bar. At 3AM you get ready to fall into bed and remember why people call high school the good-old-days. Never as the mom of a high-schooler did I feel this tired. Hey friend, you know who you are...it was great to see you tonight and chat through our open car windows. I hope our paths cross again soon, just maybe not on $2^{nd}$ Street.

*The wisdom in this story: Never drink and drive. Loving moms actually don't mind being designated drivers. Cruisin' on $2^{nd}$ Street makes them feel the most "cool" they've felt in years.*

# *Princess Friends Forever*

**Tuesday, July 18**

I was diagnosed with cancer during my oldest daughter's senior year of high school. She was always such a happy child, seeing the good in everyone. Unfortunately cancer changed that. Her world became my black and white. She learned that sometimes others aren't kind. It was a hard year for her, a time when she would most need her friends. Sadly, some of her friends turned their backs on her; it was awful. However, it was also the year that she was selected to represent the dairy industry on our State Royalty Team. It was on that team she became best friends with another dairy princess. Long after their princess reign ended, they continued to talk almost daily...princess friends forever. She surprised my daughter with a visit yesterday. When a past State Dairy Princess who also happens to be your daughter's best friend comes to visit, you get your classroom expertly organized and decorated. You get to appreciate beautiful sunsets with someone who shares your same values. You get to eat more ice cream than usual. If the cows get out, you get an extra hand in the milking parlor, even if she is wearing a cute summer romper with borrowed barn boots. If you stay up way too late talking, reminiscing, and dreaming it's really okay because Dairy Princess visits usually turn into Dairy Princess sleepovers. You get to fall asleep knowing that tomorrow will bring more opportunity for memory making. My daughter's Dairy Princess year and my cancer year coincided. At the time, I cursed cancer and said it didn't seem fair. While I still curse cancer, that one single year did teach all of us that a true friend is one who stays by your side through the best and even the worst of times.

*The wisdom in this story: A best friend is a friend who can make you laugh even when you think you'll never smile again.*

# *Tiny Treasures*

## Wednesday, July 19

My sister saves nothing, I save everything. My task today is
finding tiny treasures in stacks of old photo slides. Even if
only for today, I think my sister will be glad I save things. I
found the best photo: white picket fence childhood, barefoot
summer, short seventies sundresses, Radio Flyer wagon, and
if you look closely, my beloved Mrs. Beasley and my little red
tricycle along for the ride. I have the best sister!

*The wisdom in this story: Life in the 70's seemed simpler, but
even then my sister was looking out for me, pulling my
wagon.*

## Little Red Wagon

*"Some days we skip along, pulling our wagons with
great confidence — so full of energy that the load seems light.*

*Some days the load seems heavy and we need someone
to help us pull our wagons over the bumps in the road.*

*Some days we are just tired. We sit in our wagon
and let someone else pull us along for awhile.*

*And some days it's kind of nice to share our little red wagons with a friend.*

*As you think about yesterday, and make plans for tomorrow,
keep in mind that there will be times when you can help pull someone's
little red wagon for a while. After all, helping to pull each other's little red
wagon is what makes it possible to face the challenges the day brings."*

MARGARET KATTER

# *Playing Rough*

**Thursday, July 20**

I don't remember when I started "playing rough" with our dog, but I feel certain it was when my children were quite busy with school activities and sports and I felt as if I had neglected man's best friend all day long while I shuffled kids to their events.  It was when the house was quiet and the dog settled in at the foot of my bed.  It started with a simple belly rub but when my dog growled a bit I gave him a push.  He would bark, bite, and gnaw at my arm until I commanded "kisses," and he retreated momentarily to give me a lick on the face.  I never really liked doggy kisses, but this intermission of rough play served as his reminder that we were still friends.  My dog is now fifteen years old.  He is partially blind and nearly deaf.  His back legs have become quite crippled and he loses his balance often.  While he still settles in at the foot of my bed, it is after I assist him in getting there, always prefaced with the question "Do you want me to get you?"  Although I am certain he is in a moderate amount of pain, he has times (usually when we offer treats) when he appears playful and steady on his feet.  At night though, he is tired, and not really wanting to play.  Occasionally, a gentle shove from me will result in his usual interaction of rough play — with of course the necessary doggy kisses.  I have noticed that most of his body remains motionless as we play, his head moving in the direction of my arm as he shows his roughness.  I sometimes wonder if he realizes I notice he is crippled, much in the same way I wonder if people notice I am so changed by cancer.  Last night I gave the dog a gentle shove.  Tired eyes looked back at me.  Ok, no rough play tonight — just a belly rub.  Recalling his last belly rub was less than a week ago, I was shocked to notice two small lumps near his ribcage.  Lumps.  Gumball sized.  Oh, dear God — cancer.  Please don't tell me this dog has cancer.  Fortunately, we have a close relationship with our veterinarian, and my daughter spent time in the clinic tonight. I didn't take our dog to the clinic *(When you live on a farm, you get house calls…)* but I did briefly ask our veterinarian if he thought it could be a tumor. My question came moments after he carried a euthanized dog to a car for a lady with tears in her eyes. Perhaps he is always stoic, but he did not look overly concerned when I asked if it could be cancer. "Could be," he replied, "or in a dog his age it could just be fatty tissue." Next week our vet will make a house call and give our sweet dog a belly rub. I secretly hope the dog will bark, bite, and gnaw at his arm until I command "kisses," at which time my vet will tell me that my dog is just perfectly fine. In the meantime I honestly think I prefer not knowing. I didn't sleep well last night. When you love animals, they become family. While I know he doesn't have a lot of time left, I cannot imagine life without him.

*The wisdom in this story: Until one has loved an animal, a part of one's soul remains unawakened.*

# *China Day*

**Saturday, July 22**

Just over a month ago, my oldest daughter and I declared that the 22nd of every month would be China Day, a day when we would use my mother's Rosenthal China from the 60's. I have a niece who expressed interest in coming, so it became an open invitation for all on my mother's side. Now, *all* isn't really a large amount of people—just my sister, our spouses, our kids, and me. As kids are of dating age, it's fun to occasionally include someone's boyfriend/girlfriend into the mix of our family craziness. Today's menu included an appetizer of prosciutto wrapped mozzarella and Italian bread with light tasting oil, followed by salad, chicken parmesan, spaghetti, broiled garlic-herb zucchini, and fresh rolls. For dessert we had cupcakes, pizzelles, and a beautiful tray of peanut-butter brownies that accidently went crashing to the floor. Fortunately the pile of shattered glass wasn't the fancy china; unfortunately the brownies were not even close to being salvageable. There have already been requests for the brownies to return on the menu next month. Suffice it to say, planning a sit-down meal with several courses requires a significant amount of meal prep, but with lots of help the tasks seemed simple. Everyone seemed to really enjoy the food, but I was distracted and simply soaking in the atmosphere. I had made it very clear that this event was optional, as I didn't want anyone to feel obligated to attend. Yet, they were here— sitting around what was once my mother's dining room table—talking, laughing, and treasuring family—all while using the beautiful china.

*The wisdom in this story: Nothing is worth more than this day.*

# *So it Begins*

**Tuesday, July 25**

And so it begins again. The college stuff has been pulled out of my closet and is placed prominently in the corner of my bedroom. While my daughter delights in being organized and taking inventory of her belongings, the pile serves as a sobering reminder that very soon our lives will change yet again as she moves into her first off-campus apartment and begins her second year of college. While I am proud of her and her many accomplishments, I struggle to accept the emptiness in my heart that comes with empty closets. Many say, "but she's not far away, and comes home often," but anyone who has sent a child off to college recognizes that a child not at home changes the whole dynamic of a household.

*The wisdom in this story:  I'm gonna miss this kid and her organized piles of stuff!*

# *Power Walking*

**Wednesday, July 26**

I didn't want to admit how much my lifestyle had become sedentary since cancer. My routine of couch, chair, bed, repeat during treatment with little ambition to do more became a habit. Injury to my back/hip late in treatment had me feeling quite miserable and pain level was significant. I began to rely more heavily on use of my handicap placard *(given to me years earlier due to my hip issues)* and actually felt quite content simply parking close by and struggling to run my errands. School wasn't much different, and aside from taking my students where they needed to go throughout the building, I limited myself to one big trudge down the hallway each day to retrieve my mail. Some days, well-meaning friends brought my mail to my room, something which secretly delighted me. *Well, maybe not so secretly, as I awarded them with accolades and chocolates.* Only recently did I admit that I don't want to be "that crippled person" for the rest of my life. I continue with my weight loss program, and while I am making some good lifestyle changes, the weight loss has been somewhat stagnant. While any type exercise is difficult for me, I knew to jumpstart the weight loss again I needed to get moving. While it's hard for me to walk any distance without the strong arm of my husband or a cane, I do quite well pushing a grocery cart. I don't know exactly how or why we decided to do it, but my oldest daughter and I decided to power-walk the supercenter. We decided we would walk every single aisle of the large store, and she encouraged me each step of the way. When I started to complain about being sweaty, she reminded me sweat meant I was burning calories. In some aisles *(when I felt the need for a rest)* we browsed, and others we passed through quickly. We held our noses in the pet food aisle, and breathed deeply in the cleaning supplies sections. We speed-walked through the snack and candy

172

aisles, recognizing tossing those items into our cart would be counterproductive. We steered ourselves carefully around other physically handicapped people, some with canes and some in wheelchairs, and I said a prayer for each of them as I saw their struggles and felt their pain. I also said a prayer of thanks for my own independence. Occasionally, we had to steer around other browsing customers or employees stocking shelves. We joked that the security camera people watching us walk every aisle probably wondered what we were up to, and we giggled at the watchful eyes of the employees who saw us cover every inch of their departments. We talked about many things while we walked, and laughed often. It occurred to me that most college-age daughters would never in a million years power walk the supercenter with their tired, old mothers—but my kid is different and special—and here she was right by my side, and even enjoying it. We had so much fun! Daily walks amounted to about two miles a day, which thrilled me. For some people, two miles would be simple, but for me two miles was a huge accomplishment. The weight loss showed on the scale, and my renewed energy for parking the car just a bit further away felt incredibly good. The true test came one morning when my daughter was at work. I had a few hours to myself, and wasn't quite sure how to spend it. I have always loved to crawl into bed when the house is quiet, but on this day, I headed to the supercenter. It was quiet and not crowded in the store, and much of my cancer year flashed through my thoughts as I clung to the cart to keep myself steady. I started to feel sweaty and wanted to complain, but it felt good—adrenaline. Yes, I had made a choice to exercise instead of crawling back in bed.

*The wisdom in this story: I have the best daughter.*

# *Man's Best Friend*

**Thursday, July 27**

Big dog is old.

Big dog is old and tired.

Big dog is old, tired, and partially blind.

Big dog is old, tired, partially blind and nearly deaf.

Big dog is old, tired, partially blind, nearly deaf, and very crippled, BUT…BIG DOG <u>DOES NOT</u> HAVE CANCER!

The vet checked big dog and said occasionally older dogs develop small fatty growth areas that are not tumors. Big dog has some fatty growth areas. I wondered if jelly donuts can cause fatty growth areas in dogs, but I didn't ask.

Big dog is loyal. Big dog is resting on the bath mat while I take a shower. He cannot hear me as I emerge with a towel wrapped around myself and I know I cannot step over him without falling. I shout his name, nothing. I shake my towel in front of him, nothing. I reach down gently and pat his head to make him aware of my presence. I pray that I don't startle him, because if I do, he will likely bite me. Big dog recognizes my touch, licks me affectionately, and stares at me. I stand up slowly, and give him a gentle nudge with my foot to indicate I want him to move. Big dog moves, and follows me into the bedroom. Big dog likes to sleep, and waits for me to lift him to the bed while I am getting dressed. Before I even finish dressing, big dog is snoring. His breathing sounds heavy, labored even, and I wonder how much time we have left with him. Big dog never left my side during my illness. Big dog's name is Hunter. It is an honor to include his story in my book.

***The wisdom in this story: Dogs truly are man's best friend.***

# As the Car was Loaded

**Tuesday, August 1**

I didn't watch as the car was loaded, my husband and daughter packing her belongings for what would be a move to her first off-campus apartment. It was the night before pick-up-your-key day and she was going to take a few things down early. She wouldn't be actually living there for sixteen more days, so I really wasn't too bothered by the fact the pile of college stuff in my bedroom corner was dwindling. I didn't expect the tears that fell from my eyes when I opened the car door the next morning. The trunk and backseat were quite full, and my heart felt quite heavy. I reminded myself my once roomy mini-van had been traded for a smaller-size car, so she really wasn't taking much, it just seemed like it. Today was only pick-up-your-key day. We were just taking "a few things." My daughter was not quite ready to move out, and I most definitely was not ready to let her. We arrived at the student townhomes and learned that built in 2007, they were beautiful and quite well managed. In the rental office we met a very efficient property manager who calls herself "mom" to the kids who live there. She was impeccably dressed, more stylish than I had expected, and in spite of a full, busy office took time to smile warmly at everyone. Our pick-up-the-key entailed a sit down meeting and informative session with a jovial and enthusiastic gentleman who is called "grandpa" by some. While he didn't tell us his job title, it seemed that he is handyman and shuttle bus driver all rolled into one. He assured me that he is available to resolve any household issue that may arise. However, he seemed most proud of his role in ensuring my daughter's safe transportation to and from campus. After our meeting with "grandpa," I took a moment to soak in my surroundings, admire the stately decorated common room, and keep my emotions in check. I was certain there were tears in my eyes, but I was determined to not let

175

any leak out. Wings, my daughter has earned her wings. An impressive Dean's List GPA and responsible choices as a freshman told me I had nothing to worry about with this kid. As we entered her apartment, I took pride in helping to carry things, knowing just a short time ago I would have been far too weak to assist. While it seemed we unpacked quickly, the piles that amassed in the small living room told me we had brought more than just a few things. It felt good to sanitize and clean her bedroom, and any dust that had settled since last year's tenant's May departure quickly dissipated. As we started to unpack bags, my daughter asked me to set up her desk. I felt honored. Like me, she is meticulous with organizing and likes things a certain way. I pulled together a nice display of her special things, amidst the more functional school supplies, but not without asking for her occasional opinion. Together, we tackled every aspect of setting up the entire room. At that moment, I realized she brought mostly everything needed from home. I'm glad I didn't watch as the car was loaded the night before, as I hadn't realized just how permanent this moment might seem. I glanced around the room, and realized that her mature style closely resembled the décor I had admired in the common room. Yes, this kid has class. Gone was most every trace of her childhood, except the colorful markers neatly displayed *in rainbow order* on her desk. As we closed the door and walked out into the balmy night, I said a prayer of thanks to God for trusting me to raise such an amazing person. She is truly a gift. I'm pretty certain "mom" in the rental office and "grandpa" the shuttle bus driver recognized the same.

**The wisdom in this story: "It is the wise mother who gives her child roots and wings." (Chinese Proverb)**

# *Puddle Stompers*

### Friday, August 4

It has been raining for almost six hours. My husband is working, two of my three children are in bed and I'm home working on my book and listening to the raindrops while I wait for my middle child to return from a day trip with her cousin. Her young dog is at my feet, making it nearly impossible to stretch my legs out under the table. I've been a little melancholy lately, and just realized I've been in a bad mood most of the week. I can't explain why, I just know I feel edgy and short tempered. August is a hard month for me. Sixteen years ago, my mother passed away. While August signals the excitement of back-to-school, it also means Summer is coming to a close, and serves as a reminder of all the things I intended to complete and didn't. Lightning flashes in the sky, and our power goes out momentarily as I hear thunder in the distance. Summer storms. I feel fortunate to live in an area where there are four distinct seasons: Spring, Summer, Fall, and Winter. There are things I like (and dislike) about each season, but I have always loved the rain. When my kids were little, they were "puddle stompers." As long as there was no threat of thunder or lightning, we ran outdoors to a large puddle on our sidewalk and stomped! I can still vividly recall their chubby faces sparkling with rainwater, blue eyes looking toward the sky, and blonde hair dripping. What I remember most is their youthful laughter, yet tonight I have tears. I have heard people compare life to the seasons. I suppose it can't always be happiness and sunshine. The young dog at my feet is now awake, and I decide that I should take her outside before my daughter arrives home. It's a shame there is still thunder and lightning in the dark night sky. I'd really like to go puddle stomping.

*The wisdom in this story: Rain, rain, go away.*

# *Chocolate Frosted with Sprinkles*

### Saturday, August 5

My mother passed away sixteen years ago today. It's already past noon, and I am still in my pajamas, working furiously on my book. I feel a little numb. Sometimes I wish this day would go by without me even realizing it is the anniversary of her passing; but at other times I am grateful I had such a wonderful mother to remember. Several years ago, to help pull myself out of my usual August 5 slump, I suggested to my children that we celebrate with a "Dessert Day." We would go to all of our favorite restaurants and eat only dessert. Most days, we eat a large meal and have no room for dessert, but life is too short to skip dessert. We thoroughly enjoyed Dessert Day, with one dessert highlight being a homemade Belgian waffle complete with fruits and chocolates for dipping. Dessert day occurred for a couple of years, but for some reason we failed to keep it an annual tradition. So today, here I sit in my usual August 5 slump. Fortunately I predicted as much, and had the forethought last night to order two dozen chocolate frosted Dunkin' Donuts — with sprinkles, *of course!* Today, I will carefully arrange the donuts on my favorite white serving tray, garnish with fresh gerbera daisy flowers, and my youngest daughter will photograph them for the cover of this book. I continue to work hard at making healthy food choices, and can proudly boast a 30+ pound weight loss. So, as I indulge in a chocolate frosted kind of day, I can only hope the scales are forgiving tomorrow.

*The wisdom in this story: I remember many things about my mother. Sadly, I don't recall what kind of donut was her favorite. I'm pretty certain my kids will always remember my favorites — jelly of course, and chocolate frosted — with sprinkles!*

# *Parallel Parking*

**Tuesday, August 8**

Today I thank God for sunny skies, bright blue barrels, and big brothers with great skill and endless patience for teaching parallel parking. Most importantly, I'm thankful I get a backseat view of it all.

*The wisdom in this story: "When you look at your life, the greatest happinesses are family happinesses." (Joyce Brothers)*

# *Just Breathe*

## Wednesday, August 9

My oldest daughter and I are trying to make the most of the time we have left together before she returns to college. I asked her what she would like to do, and she suggested a visit to a salt room. The idea didn't really appeal to me, as it seemed sort of a trendy thing to do, and I'm far from trendy. I also vividly recalled hearing a story about someone falling off the chair in the salt room. Although the brochure stated the room could be somewhat cool, I envisioned a sauna, and was reminded of how much I hate to sweat. However, I wanted to do what my daughter wanted to do, so I scheduled an appointment for us. The idea of this day was for us to relax a bit, but just the thought of the salt room was causing me a slight bit of anxiety. That all lessened as soon as we arrived at the wellness center. A stack of small and outdated lockers in the waiting room beckoned for us to remove our shoes, but otherwise we entered the room in our regular clothing, *thank goodness.* Anything requiring me to change clothes and use a locker was strangely reminiscent of my many visits to medical facilities. As we entered the dimly lit room, the crushed salt at my feet felt wonderful. I walked slowly to a chair in the furthest corner of the room, and smiled as I sat down carefully. Feet firmly in the salt, I cautiously started to tilt back in the zero gravity chair—so far, so good. My daughter reclined quickly, pulled a blanket over herself, and politely reminded me the wellness center enforced a no talking policy. As the salt machine started blowing a delicate dusting of salt into in the air, *(or at least I think that's how it works)* I tried to relax. I heard a faint bit of music in the distance, but the whir of the machine seemed to overpower it. I focused my eyes on the salted ceiling above, and the speckled green lights that danced across the room like twinkling stars. Green—why *green* lights? The green was pretty, but I thought perhaps a blue would have been more appropriate, or a purple more calming. My mind wandered to the light bulb that filtered the speckled green and I realized I was analyzing this place much in the same way I analyzed the hospital rooms in which I awaited surgical procedures. *Relax, Michele, relax.* I whispered to my daughter, "I like it here, what do you think?" She smiled and nodded. My rule-following daughter was careful not to speak. She closed her eyes again, and pulled the blanket a little closer to her chin. I tapped her gently. "I think your sister would like it here." Again, she nodded. I added, "It's hard for me to sit still. I think your sister might have trouble sitting still. I saw buckets in the other corner. I suppose she could play with salt in the buckets." I assumed the buckets were primarily meant for toddlers, and thought how silly it might seem for my sixteen-year-old to seat herself on the floor to play in the salt room. Then I wondered if perhaps the woman who fell out of the chair was trying to sit on the floor to play in the salt room. I stifled a laugh and closed my eyes. I whispered to my daughter a few more times and then perceived that although she would never say it, my interruptions were surely intruding on her time to relax. At this point, I felt certain at least 20 minutes of our 45-minute session had passed. I wondered briefly why it was so hard for me to sit still, and my mind then started to wonder about the benefits of the salt room. The wellness center brochure boasts salt caves have a positive influence on mental and physical health. Apparently breathing the salt filled air allows us to think more clearly, sleep more soundly, and stay healthier. The sentence about making guests feel young and rejuvenated made me laugh a little, and I wondered if all adults are tempted to play with the salt in the little buckets or just me. As I sat in a room full of imported Dead Sea salt, I decided if the effects truly were clearer sinuses, I needed to focus on my breathing. With my first deep breath, I was reminded of my deep breaths during radiation treatments. It was hard for me to inhale without counting, and I hesitated before exhaling, remembering times during radiation treatment when someone had to tell me it was okay to do so before I could again breathe normally. I rested my hands on my chest and felt the rise and fall of each deep breath I took. After a few deep breaths, I considered how shallow my normal breathing really is, and I wondered if my fast paced life is a detriment to my health. At some point, the music seemed louder and amidst the soft piano notes I heard a whooshing of ocean waves. Yes, this was most definitely a relaxing place. I wanted to whisper to my daughter, but she looked peaceful, calm, and relaxed. I focused on my breathing, the music, and the twinkling green lights. It was hard to describe how I was starting to feel. The word *zen* came to mind, but I think zen is a trendy word and I'm far from trendy. I thought about the definition of zen, and I knew it exactly, as I had looked it up once when my younger daughter attended her yoga class. Zen is defined as:

*"a state of focus that incorporates total togetherness of body & mind."*

Yes, I was most definitely feeling zen. The larger light in the room came back on, a signal our session had ended. My outstretched body was finally peaceful, calm, and relaxed. It took awhile, but I had learned to *just breathe.* I wished we could stay a little longer. I returned the chair to seated position, and carefully stood. As I walked across the thick salt filled floor, I thought of the lady who fell off the chair. *(How exactly did she fall off the chair?)* I giggled and retrieved my shoes from the locker. My daughter and I decided we wanted to return another day. I bought a ten-pass punch card. I think my younger daughter will want to come along. Maybe we can sit in the corner and play with the buckets.

**The wisdom in this story: "You should sit in meditation for 20 minutes a day, unless you're too busy; then you should sit for an hour." (Old Zen saying)**

# *Sleep the Day Away*

**Friday, August 11**

I have never been a morning person. I love to lie in bed and
wake up slowly, listening to the sounds around me, and
thinking about the day that awaits me. One of my favorite
memories of childhood was hearing my mother pull my
bedroom door shut tightly to block out any noise from others
who were already awake and starting their day. She was
always respectful of anyone who was asleep, and could often
be heard saying, "let her sleep" if someone questioned why
one of the tired teenagers in our home was still in bed. My
father loved to cook, and the waft of bacon filling the hallways
of our home prompted me to eventually retreat to the kitchen
where he lovingly prepared eggs-to-order. The smell of coffee
still reminds me of my parents, who each enjoyed a cup daily.
Although I am now the adult, today is no different, and I am
struggling to be a morning person. It has been raining, and
nothing on the calendar requires me to rise early. My
husband has pulled our bedroom door shut, and I lie here
waking up slowly, thinking about the day that awaits me. I
listen to the sounds in my own home, and miss having a mom
to shush out the noise. Even with my door shut, I hear the
echo of voices in the kitchen, loud music playing, and the
barking of three dogs. I wonder for a moment why I ever
agreed to three dogs. I hear the clink of a mop and the smell
of bleach, recognizing I am fortunate to have a husband who
is willing to clean — especially when I am still in bed. I am
thinking about the sounds I am hearing — happy sounds — and
decide I'm ready to get up and greet the day God has given
me, but not before the door bursts open and a fluffy white
puppy jumps on my bed. My oldest daughter *(who is very
much a morning person)* greets me with a cheerful "Good
morning," and when I tell her I'm finally getting up *(It's only
8:30 a.m.)* she responds, "Oh, good! I don't know why anyone

would want to just sleep the day away." I tell my daughter to "let her sister sleep" when she starts to enter that bedroom with a puppy in her arms. She knows not to wake her brother. I shower quickly and join my husband in the kitchen. The couch looks tempting, but I fear if I sit I won't want to get up. Instead, I take a look at the calendar and begin planning my week. I'm tired just thinking about the events to come during this busy end-of-summer. I wonder what fueled my parents. Was it the coffee—straight black, the promise of eggs and bacon, or simply their incredible zest for life? My husband and daughter exchange words, and although the music drowns out what they are saying, laughter ensues. All three dogs appear to be playing, and the tired old dog has a ball in his mouth. I love my warm bed, but even more so, I love my happy home—my happy life. I look back at my to-do list with renewed energy. I have a few errands to run today. I think I'm headed to the grocery store first—we need some bacon.

**The wisdom in this story:  Wake up and smell the bacon.**

# *It's Not Nothing*

## Wednesday, August 16

"It's not nothing." Yes, this is how I felt as the tears fell from my eyes on my drive home from my daughter's college apartment last evening. The events of the day unfolded slowly, and while I delighted in our time together it seemed to prolong the inevitable—she had somewhere else to call home. I liked and disliked all at once the quote on the picture frame I gave her: "Home is where you drop your anchor." I think the frame was meant to be beach house décor, but the saying seemed fitting for a girl at a college whose logo included a sailboat. She will fill the frame with a photo of her roommates, and place it alongside the other photos that tell the story of her life. I felt her warm embrace, watched her hug her sister and dad, and I cussed a little that big brother hadn't come along for this farewell. I sat quietly in the car and watched as my husband dutifully snapped the photograph I requested of her standing by the front door. I listened intently and found joy in hearing the enthusiastic greeting of her roommates as she entered the apartment. Then the door closed...my signal to leave. While her newfound independence is very well deserved, it doesn't make parting any easier. The tears started flowing as soon as my car turned the corner. Without even realizing I was preparing to speak, the words "I just like it best when you're all at home" came from my mouth and likely puzzled bewildered little sister in the passenger seat. My husband had driven separately, and for a moment I thought it best, as I knew his eyes were glistening, too. While I felt a little embarrassed at my own emotion, I read an online article this morning that helped to justify my feelings. The author writes about how very hard it is to see our children walk out the door. She recognizes it's not the end of the world, but it is the end of the familiarity that comes in a life filled with shuffling children to activities, making meals, and offering an opinion to someone still young enough to want to hear it.  She talks about sharing in their ideas and dreams, and having a home where friends are comfortable coming and going.  She talks about always.  "Always is what you miss.  Always knowing where they are—at school, at practice, at a friend's house."  The wisdom in this story touched me deeply.  It's a great thought if someone in your life has a new place to drop his or her anchor.

*The wisdom in this story:  "It's not a death.  And it's not a tragedy.  But it's not nothing either.*

# Driver's License Brownies

## Thursday, August 17

When my nephew got his driver's license in 2008 it was a momentous occasion. To help him celebrate, I painstakingly made a large size version of his license and placed it atop a cake. It was a hit! Subsequently I decorated cakes or brownies for my son, daughter, other relatives, and friends. The stipulation was always that new drivers needed to drive to my house solo to receive the treat. Today, I told my youngest daughter her brownies would be a little tricky due to our state's new license design. She told me not to worry about it, to buy a cupcake and stick her real license in it. We bought some cupcakes, but no one was home to celebrate so we said we would enjoy them tomorrow. She went to bed hours ago. Sleep eluded me. It's now almost midnight and I just took fresh brownies from the oven. A large size license replica will be a wonderful breakfast surprise. Someone asked where she would travel solo first... gymnastics, of course. Sometimes I think she lives in the gym. Congratulations to my new driver! I love you and I am proud of you. Have fun and be safe.

*The wisdom in this story: Twenty-one years of driving kids. Now I simply sit back and let them take the wheel. Life is good.*

# *Gentle Touch*

### Friday, August 18

Shortly after treatment ended, my doctor recommended I go for lymphedema therapy. Swelling and discomfort following the removal of lymph nodes is not uncommon. While I had swelling and discomfort, I just wanted to be done — done with missed work, done with appointments, done with cancer. My body had been cut, infused with chemo, and radiated. I needed a little break. Unfortunately, my decision to refuse therapy wasn't the best one. I didn't realize how much the benefits of therapy could improve the quality of my life. I had nights when turning onto my side woke me, days when the pain seemed unbearable, and moments when the slightest bump from an elementary student traveling too fast in the hallway caused me to cringe. During the day, I walked around school protecting my breast, using my lesson plan book like a shield. I kept busy to avoid the discomfort. At night, I prayed restless tossing and turning wouldn't cause pain. At times frustration got the best of me and I cried. Nearly one year after finishing treatment, I decided perhaps I would indeed *try* this therapy. *I wasn't going to like it, and I knew that much.* The appointments would cause me to return to the cancer center, a place I truly loved to hate. I thrived in being busy, and "who has time for therapy" was my motto. However, I knew I needed to *make* time if I wanted any relief from my discomfort. My first appointment was during Spring vacation from school, and scheduled so I wouldn't have to miss a day of work. The therapist, while pleasant, was a stranger to me — and just one more person who would see me unclothed and wearing one of the hideous gowns hospitals seem to select. A gown that stole my modesty, a gown that once again would label me as a patient — a sick person. Upon meeting the therapist, I decided immediately that I liked her, and remember — my world is of only black and white and I either like you or I don't *(not my best trait)*. The therapist started our visit by showing posters of the lymph channels and offering a brief science lesson of how the lymphatic system helps to drain the body of toxins and fluids. I didn't tell her how much I dislike science, but rather listened intently trying to understand why my breast and armpit were so tender. The science lesson helped to ease some of the awkward tension I felt in thinking *"I'm here for a boob massage."* I learned that it wasn't a boob massage, but rather a slow and gentle process of encouraging the lymphatic fluids to flow in the right direction and ease discomfort. The dim lights, her gentle touch, and soft voice helped me to relax — but I was a skeptic. *Really*, was her touch *really* able to lesson the swelling in some magical way? Briefly regretting I hadn't paid more attention in high school and college science classes, I lie there wondering how the body really does work, and praying her gentle touch was worth my time and thirty-five dollar co-pay. She learned I was a teacher, and we spent the hour talking about school, my children, and her children with a bit of cancer talk thrown in for good measure. I learned in addition to her physical therapy credentials, she also has a psychology background — something I suppose is essential in working with troubled post-cancer patients. The hour passed quickly and I went home feeling optimistic. By evening, I imagined I truly was feeling better — but remember I'm a skeptic so I thought it couldn't be true. I returned weekly, and those appointments brought me unbelievable comfort. My husband accompanied me to one appointment and she ever so patiently taught him all he needed to know for a proper lymphatic massage *(so I could be treated without the dreaded co-pay)*. While my husband tried, massage wasn't something for which we made time. I ended up deciding his role as caregiver deserved a hiatus as much as I deserved a hiatus from being a cancer patient. My therapy would continue with the professional. The cost of a co-pay went from a stressful amount to a worth-every-penny expenditure. After each treatment I felt a little better, first noticing a decrease in pain during the day and eventually being able to sleep on my side without discomfort at night. I became a firm believer in lymphatic massage, and scolded myself for not going sooner. At some point, and I'm not sure when, my therapist started giving me a warm hug at the end of each appointment. She had become not just a physical therapist or psychologist, but rather my friend. She worked at the place I loved to hate, and like everyone else there, I was thankful for her presence in my life. I treasured this time with her. With every gentle touch, she has helped me to heal. School will start again soon, and my appointments will become less frequent. Today, I told her about my recently diagnosed friend — *told her cancer sucks* — and she shared a story about someone in her life recently diagnosed, too. We both had tears in our eyes, and I was again reminded of how much respect I have for healthcare professionals. Therapy has improved the quality of my life, both emotional and physical. For that, I feel blessed and extremely grateful.

**The wisdom in this story: "Touch the body. Calm the mind. Heal the spirit." (unknown)**

# *Glazed Goodness*

**Saturday, August 19**

"I didn't really have much of a summer," lamented my youngest daughter. No—between taking an advanced math class, countless hours at gymnastics practice, and volunteering twice a week in a vet clinic—she *didn't* have much of a summer. Gone are the lazy, hazy days we once knew and loved. When my children were small, we always celebrated the end of summer with a "last hurrah." We even called it our last hurrah, and there was a big to-do about planning the events of the day. Fast forward to now: My son works full time year-round, so there is no last hurrah for him. My daughters never seemed to both be home at the same time, so we planned nothing really special together before summer escaped from our grasp. So here it is, the last Saturday before back to school, and we are both feeling a little melancholy. She has a special plan for our day, and it involves donuts. I'm not sure of the fine line in which an affinity for something becomes an addiction, but I'm fairly certain we are both addicted to donuts. Last Spring in another part of the state, we discovered a donut shop where freshly made donuts are served still warm when the light is on—a very new concept to all of us. The shop is a franchise, and determined to find the location nearest our home; we did a quick online search. Exactly sixty-seven miles, approximately one hour thirteen minutes, separated us from such glazed goodness. Who in the world would travel sixty-seven miles and across a state border for a donut? Well, we've been there once already. This weekend, in honor of the upcoming solar eclipse, the donut shop will fill their intricate glaze machine with *chocolate* glaze. Yes, this would most definitely be a reason to return to the donut shop, and I couldn't think of a more appropriate last hurrah to our summer. The chocolate glaze doesn't start flowing until 4PM and at the moment; my daughter is at a friend's house making tie-dye shirts to be worn on the second day of school, a tradition for most students. Earlier this morning, as I reflected on her "I didn't really have much of a summer" comment, I suggested perhaps her friends might want to come along to the donut shop. I reminded her they needed to know it was sixty-seven miles away. As happens with good friends, they responded with a resoundingly enthusiast yes — they wanted to come along. I asked her if they had ever been there. She replied, "No, but I told them they have the best donuts in the world." Affinity? Addiction? Most definitely addiction — and she is most definitely my daughter. No one else shares our exact enthusiasm for food. What started as a melancholy Saturday is going to become a fabulous last hurrah.

*The wisdom in this story: Donuts taste even better when shared with a friend.*

# *Hugs and Kisses*

## Sunday, August 27

I once dated a boy whose family I also grew to love. I spent a lot of time at his house, and with each departure I gave his sweet mom a hug goodbye. The boy received a *really quick* kiss before I got in my car, because goodness—someone might be looking out the window, and I was *not* one to display my affections publicly. I was young—a college girl, the boy— already working a full time job, and we both had a bit of difficulty deciding we were ready to commit to a serious relationship. We were both strong-willed, both had a bit of a stubborn temper, and neither of us willing to address our shortcomings. It's quite possible we set a record for the number of break-ups and get-back-together times, but thankfully I chose not to keep count. However, I do vividly recall one of the breakups and a time of saying farewell to his mother. I was fairly certain it was over this time "for good" — and I wanted to rid his life of every last trace of me. I insisted he give back every single thing I had given him—every photograph, card, and letter lovingly sent from the big blue mailbox outside of the college dining hall—everything, which I later tore into shreds. His mother had placed everything in a large shopping bag, and I stood on her front porch ready to retrieve it all, but secretly wondering if we weren't worth one more try. His mother and I both had tears in our eyes, and she hugged me tightly. Her words that followed surprised me a bit, "You are the one who taught me to hug." Oh my—I wasn't sure how to respond to this—as my own mom loved hugs and hugs came quite naturally to me. How had this lady raised four incredible kids without knowing the loving feeling of a hug? They were a busy farm family, and she had a huge garden to tend to, so perhaps the hugs just became lost in the shuffle. I didn't question, but instead felt honored that I had touched her life, even if in just this one small way. More than a year passed, and eventually this young boy and I decided we were worth one more try. I regretted shredding all of the photographs, cards, and letters and delighted in the one photo that had fallen to the sidewalk when I left, which was retrieved and saved by his mother. A few years after that, I married him. Early days in our marriage were filled with hugs and kisses. We had children. I delighted in teaching them to hug and kiss. There is nothing more precious than blowing kisses to a toddler and having them send one back to you in return. Our home was filled with love, and visits to my husband's childhood home frequent. With each departure after a visit, his mother reached out to hug me farewell. As I juggled diaper bags, kids, and leftovers of her home-cooked meals, I occasionally rushed out the door without reaching out to her. The hugs became a little less frequent. My toddlers grew into teenagers, and there was nothing more uncool than hugging and kissing your mother — except maybe hugging your brother. My kids were quick to greet friends with the warm embrace of a hug, but became much more distant with loved ones. I didn't push the issue, as we all knew the love was there, perhaps the affection wasn't as important. Even the "blow me a kiss" of their toddler days became a fast *mwwahh* exhale from their mouths as they tried not to roll their eyes in disgust. Cancer entered our lives, and my husband and I started hugging more frequently. I don't really think it was hugging but rather him holding me up keeping me strong, at times when I felt everything in my world was falling apart. One day last week, our kitchen was filled with laughter. I can't remember what prompted it, but it felt good. I smiled and my husband's bewildered look in return made me laugh a little. Such happiness had not been with us during the darkest days of cancer. My husband put his arms around me, and I realized how much I missed the warmth we once shared. My oldest daughter giggled and said, "Do you remember when you two used to hug and I squeezed in between you?" It was a memory faded by time, but yes, I remembered. It happened often. Every time my husband closed in for a warm embrace, we felt the tugging hands of a child who wanted to be a part of our love. When had this stopped? I didn't want to believe that we had become a family that didn't regularly hug and kiss — but that is exactly what we had become. Christmas is coming soon. I have one thing on my Christmas list. Even if they roll their eyes in disgust, we will again learn to hug and kiss — and if they forget how, there's a sweet lady next door who can surely teach them.

*The wisdom in this story: Hugging is a silent way of saying, "You matter to me."*

# *To the Moon and Back*

## Thursday, August 31

In 1994, the book *Guess How Much I Love You* written by Sam McBratney and illustrated by Anita Jeram was published.

In 1996, my first child was born. I loved reading *Guess How Much I Love You* to him. It was one of my favorite books.

In 1998, my second child was born. She delighted in looking at pictures of Little Nutbrown Hare and I could recite the entire story without even looking at the words.

By the year 2000, when I was pregnant with my third child the book was printed in big book format. I remember sitting on the floor reading *Guess How Much I Love You* to all three of my children, and realized perhaps I liked the book more than they did. It was my favorite, but not theirs — to the moon and back.

I'm not sure when, but in what seemed like an instant, a quote from the book *"I love you right up to the moon – and back"* became emblazoned on everything. Products ranged from nursery bedding to clothing, note cards and home décor. The books became available in all sizes and with gift editions. "I love you right up to the moon — and back," was a phrase that became commercialized and no longer a private sentiment I shared with my children. It had become too popular...cliché.

By the year 2017, *Guess How Much I Love You* had been translated into 53 languages, and 28 million units had been sold. My children were practically all grown up at the ages of 21, 18, and 16 — and the stories of Little Nutbrown Hare long since forgotten. We never really talked about the phrase, "I love you right up to the moon — and back" and I wondered if they, too thought it was something cliché they saw in stores. However cliché it seemed to me, the book became a bestseller and touched lives deeply. The author of the book attributes the success of *Guess How Much I Love You* to the simplicity of the words. He states, "The words are simple, direct, and true."

A few days ago, we received some awful news. The older sister of my daughter's best friend had passed away suddenly. Hers was a life too short, and her family was devastated. The funeral date was set and my heart ached. My thoughts turned to another recent funeral, and a conversation I had with my young son about the importance of attending funerals to support loved ones in difficult times. My son, wise and mature beyond his years, didn't really need the explanation. I think I was speaking those words to reassure myself. Yet, this time things seemed different. My youngest, my baby, had never attended a funeral. I wanted to wrap her in my arms and protect her from the harsh reality of loss; and yet, her best friend surely needed her. I decided we would attend the funeral. We made plans to join another mother/daughter and with a heavy heart, I encouraged my daughter to sign the sympathy card herself. I added a favorite book *The Gift of a Memory (Marianne Richmond)* and prayed it would bring them some comfort in the difficult days ahead. The sky seemed ominous on the way to the funeral, sun shining brightly but raindrops falling gently, and I caught myself wondering out loud if Heaven does truly try to speak to us through the glorious colors of the sky. My daughter informed us we were simply "driving into a storm" and I thought those words alone seemed like a metaphor. Nothing prepared me for greeting the tearful family members and the heartbreaking yet heartwarming service that followed. I sat in a pew with other mothers and daughters and we all struggled to keep our composure. Beautiful stories were shared about the girl so very loved by her family and gone too soon. As we departed the sanctuary, elaborate photo displays, fresh cut flowers, and wooden plaques adorned the church hallway. The plaques were simple, direct, and true:

*"I love you right up to the moon – and back."*

My thoughts immediately rushed back to the days of long ago, and the words I once whispered to my own children as we gathered around the big book *Guess How Much I Love You*. Such simple, direct, and true words would now have to carry this family thorough some of their most difficult days. I glanced at photos of their little girl, and imagined her wide eyes once delighting in the stories of Little Nutbrown Hare. I wondered if they too, could recite the entire story without even looking at the words. I wondered if, even as the words became too cliché, they were words treasured by this special family. I looked at my own daughter, and noticed the awkward silence she shared with her typically silly friends, the harsh reality of loss now etched in their minds. At that moment, I wanted to whisk her away, and yet I couldn't have been more proud of these young ladies. Showing love and compassion to a friend who surely needed them…that is what this life is all about, and they are learning it at a young age. As we walked out into the stillness of the night, I looked at the early night sky above. My eyes were drawn to some swiftly moving clouds, and as they passed through, a bright shiny moon was revealed. I took a deep breath and blinked rapidly to prevent the tears from flowing. Yes, I do believe Heaven does truly speak to us through the glorious colors of the sky. The moon—tonight's moon *(just four nights away from being a full moon)* spoke volumes.
**The wisdom in this story: I think "Guess How Much I Love You" is still one of my favorite books. I need to share it with my children.**

# *Dream Machine Refurbished*

## Saturday, September 2

The year was 1993, and I was engaged to be married. My husband-to-be disliked shopping, so my mother and I shopped to select items for our new home. We bought essentials, but contemplated and commiserated before making any purchase that seemed frivolous or inessential. We were "Outlet Center" shoppers, and as we arrived at a local outlet, I was thrilled to see a Sony store. Sony Corporation was quite trendy among young people, and I was immediately drawn to an alarm clock radio known as the Sony Dream Machine. This clock radio offered two independent alarm settings, perfect for a newly married couple that would rise and sleep at different times. Wake options were buzz or radio, and it had a snooze button. Yes, I *wanted* that radio. The price *was* a bit steep, but it would be an important purchase, and surely Sony was worth the splurge. My mother waited in the car while I ran in the store quickly, and returned with a Dream Machine in hand. I was proud of my purchase, and eager to show it to her. However, my smile softened when she disappointedly exclaimed *"Refurbished?!?* Michele, you *don't* want something that is *refurbished."* Well, refurbished was simply what was in my budget and what I was willing to spend on an alarm clock. My mother didn't think refurbished was a good idea, and when my mother said something wasn't a good idea — *it wasn't a good idea.* She encouraged me to return it. She would pay the difference for a new one. Nope. Sony knew all about people like me, the impulse buyers. Final sale. No returns were accepted on *refurbished* items. Placing the Dream Machine on my nightstand felt a little bittersweet, but it looked nice — sleek, black, and modern. Early in my marriage I sometimes wondered if the alarm might stop working and cause us to oversleep and be late to work. However, the beloved Sony kept on buzzing and snoozing with us through the years. As young parents we set our alarms faithfully, but really didn't need them as most days young children woke us long before the alarm. I cussed at the alarm when my oldest started middle school, but that Sony helped me get out of bed early enough to make dippy eggs for my son before he boarded the 6:32 AM school bus. A few years later, all three of my children became fairly self-sufficient and I started to really like the snooze button. Each morning, I pulled the blankets up around me and snuggled in a little tighter, the Dream Machine never failing to offer as many wake up reminders as needed. Then cancer came. My sleep became terribly interrupted. During the nighttime hours, I was awake—almost every single hour. I watched the numbers on the Dream Machine change, dozed a bit, and awoke just moments later to see they hadn't changed much at all. One night, in a fit of sleeplessness, I heard a humming static sound, much like that of a radio station out of range. I checked the alarm. It was still set correctly. I turned on the radio. The station was clear. The mysterious sound stopped. I was pretty certain my Dream Machine was dying a slow death. *Damn refurbished.* When morning came, the alarm went off just as it should. All was quiet the next night, and the alarm continued to work normally. Weeks later, I heard the sound again. One evening, my husband noticed it. Now, months later, I have heard the humming static sound approximately 10 times. Sometimes the strange sound brings me comfort. Sony has manufactured an incredible product that has lasted almost 25 years and still wakes me every single morning without fail. I believe angels are among us. I believe that sometimes, *even if it is in a very strange way*, my mother is making her presence in my life known. I am pretty certain she is trying to tell me my damn refurbished Dream Machine was a smart purchase.

*The wisdom in this story: Buy refurbished.*

# *As We Are*

## Sunday, September 10

Twenty panes of glass and a six-pane transom make up the window that serves as my current view of a peacefully trickling fountain. Plush cushioned casual seating for eight and beautiful stained glass décor make this quiet room feel like home, only slightly better. A soft yet pungent waft of grapefruit and vanilla are vented into the room, and a bowl of chocolates both dark and milk is placed strategically on a side table. Two glass-paneled doors offset at angles in the room add to the style in a way only one who loves architecture can appreciate. Everything around me — the wicker furniture, the upholstery fabric, even the handrail on the staircase I see through the window is not surprisingly a variant shade of mocha. Tall white pillars add to the grandeur of an otherwise simple room. A hallway table nearby has fruited ice water readily available for anyone wishing to dispense it. A bowl of fresh apples and assorted trail mix seem the perfect healthy accompaniment to the blueberry crumb, lemon poppy seed, and chocolate fudge muffins that seem irresistible. *Jelly Donut Days*, perfect reading material for this quiet reflective day is on my lap, and my newly polished toes seem to glisten. I have spent the day simply being alive and soaking in my surroundings. We are at the spa, celebrating my oldest daughter's nineteenth birthday. Little sister is along this time, and we are finding joy in her company. This is her first visit to the spa, so she looks at it through fresh eyes. While she is impressed, her youth is evident as she has difficulty being still and quiet. In time, she will find joy in the solitude, but for now she is content eating chocolate. For me, it is a privilege to be here, and I am feeling pampered. Once again, I quietly wonder why my own mother never afforded herself such luxury, but remind myself that while she treated her children, she never treated herself. I do some mental math to calculate the cost of this day with my girls, and regret for a moment that with bills to pay this is how I am choosing to spend money. The regret lasts only for a moment though, as the strong aroma of some freshly dispensed dark hot cocoa reawakens my senses. Small sips warm my tummy and my heart. Like the beach, the spa has become my happy place. As I wrap my hands around the warm mug, I give thanks that my husband smiles and tells us to indulge on occasion when my daughters and I mention planning a trip to the spa. For it is here that I feel most able to reflect on my life. I vividly recall shortly after diagnosis someone telling me cancer would change my life. Those words made me angry. I liked my life. I loved my life. My life was probably as close to perfect as perfect can be. Cancer crashed my world. Cancer made me bitter. I fought hard, and found my happy ending after treatment, but not without a lot of battle scars. Tears flow more easily now; sometimes to the point it concerns me. I hurt for those who are newly diagnosed, for those fighting the fight, and for those who have sadly passed. Cancer has changed me. Cancer has changed my life. It has become part of my story. A young musician recently recorded a beautiful thought provoking song titled *Stand in the Light*. When interviewed about the meaning of the song, he remarked, "The greatest risk you can take is just being yourself and being seen as you are." The lyrics of his song are full of wisdom:

1. *"This is who I am inside. I'm not going to hide."*
2. *"Never look back as you're walking away."*
3. *"Carry the music, the memories, and keep them inside."*
4. *"Laugh every day."*
5. *"Don't stop those tears from falling down."*
6. *"With courage and kindness hold onto your faith."*
7. *"Climb up leaving sadness behind you."*
8. *"Fight hard for love, we can never give enough.*

*The wisdom in this story:*

*"Stand in the light and be seen as we are."*
*(Jordan Smith)*

*Michele's e-mail:*

*jellydonutdays@gmail.com*

# These are a few of my favorite things:

| |
|---|
| **www.band-aid.com**<br>*America's #1 bandage.* |
| **www.broadway.com**<br>*Keep a show tune in your heart.* |
| **www.crayolaexperience.com**<br>*Color, sculpt, and paint to your heart's content.* |
| **www.dunkindonuts.com**<br>*Buy the chocolate frosted…with sprinkles!* |
| **www.guesshowmuchiloveyou.com**<br>*For those you love right up to the moon--& back.* |
| **www.hersheyspa.com**<br>*Sweet Feet pedicures are the best!* |
| **www.jif.com**<br>*Choosy mothers choose Jif.* |
| **www.jordansmithofficial.com**<br>*Stand in the Light is my new favorite song.* |
| **www.kleenex.com**<br>*Show you care.* |
| **www.krispykreme.com**<br>*Be sure to go when the light is shining brightly.* |
| **www.mariannerichmond.com**<br>*The author of many of my favorite books.* |
| **www.pabreastcancer.org**<br>*A cancer organization dear to my heart.* |
| **www.pbs.org**<br>*Snuggle up with your own little monkey.* |
| **www.puffs.com**<br>*I recommend Puffs Plus Lotion.* |
| **www.sony.com**<br>*Sony Dream Machine – an oldie but goodie!* |
| **www.weightwatchers.com**<br>*In remembering my "why", I'll lose the weight.* |

Coming Soon

# LOVE, HUGS, AND CHEESEBURGERS
*Life after Breast Cancer, Cherish Every Single Day*